LUKE

LUKE

James and Audrey Bentley

Contents

1 A man named Luke   **1**

What was Luke like?   *1*
Reading people's minds   1
Luke's hero   2
Four portraits of Jesus   2

A 'gospel'   *2*
Good news for the downtrodden   5
Few believed Jesus   6
Luke the passionate believer   6

Can we trust Luke?   *7*
Luke used Mark's gospel   7
   How Jesus healed a leper
Other gospels?   9
Some things Luke alone tells us   9

Oral tradition   *10*
Changing the point   10
   An example: the withered fig
   tree
When did Luke write his gospel?   12
Luke the careful historian   12

Essential information about Luke   *14*
What Paul tells us about Luke   14
Doctor Luke?   14
A non-Jew?   15

A Gentile's concerns   *16*
The gospel is for everyone   16
   Theophilus
   Jesus's family tree
   Seventy missionaries
   Good Gentiles, ready to
   believe
Christians are good citizens   17

The Romans found Jesus
innocent
The parable of the coin and
the tribute money
The Roman soldier at the
crucifixion

Assignments   *20*

2 The coming of the Son of God   **22**

The angel Gabriel brings a
message to Mary   *22*
What does 'Jesus' mean?   22

Son of God   *23*
The baptism of Jesus   23
The transfiguration of Jesus   24

'Son of God' and 'Son of man'   *25*
The virgin birth   26
Mary visits Elizabeth   26

Bethlehem   *27*
Jesus is born in a stable   28
An angel tells shepherds about
the birth of Jesus   30
The shepherds worship Jesus   31
Christmas   32
   The two faces of Christmas

The angel's names for Jesus   *33*
Saviour   33
Christ   34
Lord   35

Assignments   *37*

3 Luke's Jesus   **39**

*Looking at people through
different eyes*   *39*
The gospel writers' views   39

Luke's own picture of Jesus   *41*
Jesus's love for the poor and
lowly   41
Jesus's attitude to the rich   42
   The absurd desire for
   possessions
   Dives and Lazarus
The power of prayer   46
Jesus teaches his followers to
pray   48
The Lord's prayer   48
   Father
   Let God's name be holy
   And let his kingdom come
   Our daily bread
   Forgiveness
   Temptation
Jesus and outcasts   52
Jesus and women   53
   Martha and Mary
   The forgiven prostitute

Assignments   *58*

4 Friends and enemies of Jesus   **60**

John the Baptist   *60*

Levi the tax collector   *60*
Leaving everything behind   62

Apostles and disciples   *62*
Jesus's real family   63

The cost of following Jesus   *63*
A new way of life   64
Disciples will be rejected, as
Jesus was   64
Homeless too   65
Even put to death   65

Those who reject Jesus   *65*
The scribes   65
The Pharisees   66
   The Pharisees and the sabbath
   The Sadducees
The religious leaders of the Jews   67
The Samaritans   68
The Romans   69
   Herod Antipas
   Pontius Pilate

Where did it all take place?   *69*
In the synagogues   69
In the Jerusalem Temple   70

Assignments   *71*

5 The teaching of Jesus   **73**

*Jesus teaches by means of
miracles*   *73*
Another nature miracle   74
Jesus's miracles display the
majesty of God   75
   Beelzebul versus the finger of
   God
A taste of the heavenly banquet   75

Lord over death   *76*
Faith and miracles   77
Healing a leper   77
The faith of a blind beggar   78
Jesus heals the mentally ill   78
Compassion and the miracles of
Jesus   79

*The central meaning of Jesus's
miracles*   *81*

Teaching in parables   *81*
   The blind leading the blind
   Taking a speck from your
   brother's eye

Parables found only in Luke   *82*
Everyday parallels   83
An acted parable   83
The good Samaritan   85

Allegories   86

Sayings   87
Conflict, judgment and promise   88
Sayings and parables   88
The new versus the old   88
Wandering sayings   89

Parables of the kingdom of God   89
Seek the kingdom above all
things   90
The great banquet   90
The kingdom of God and this
world   91
The kingdom and Jesus's second
coming   92
The kingdom of God is near   93
The kingdom and the Church   93
Beatitudes and woes   95
    The blessed
    Woes
    No limits to love
    The merciful sons of the Most
    High

Assignments   97

6 The way of the cross   102

*A sword shall pierce Mary's
heart*   102
False ways rejected by Jesus   102

Jesus in conflict   103
Lord of the sabbath   103
What are laws for?   104
Two more healings bring both
love and hatred for Jesus   104
    A sick woman in a synagogue
    A man with dropsy
An attempt to kill Jesus at
Nazareth   105

He went his way   105
Riding into Jerusalem   107
Jerusalem and its Temple   107
Jesus cleanses the Temple   108

Judas agrees to betray Jesus   108
The Last Supper   109
Serving, obeying and betraying   110

The trials of Jesus   111
The charges   111
    Before the Jewish Council
    Before Herod Antipas
    Before Pontius Pilate

Jesus is crucified   113
Jesus forgives while hanging on
the cross   113
Dead and buried   113
Deeper meanings   114
Fulfilling the promises of the
prophets   115

The empty tomb   115
The road to Emmaus   115
Jesus has appeared to Simon   116
A real person   116
The mission of the disciples   116

Jesus's final journey   117
Joy   117
Heaven   117
Worship   117

Assignments   118

General questions   121

7 A detailed breakdown of Luke's gospel   124

Introduction   124
The beginning of the age of the
Messiah   124
Jesus's ministry begins   124
The Messiah in action   124
The teachings of Jesus   125
Miracles and teaching   125
Who is Jesus?   125
Following or rejecting Jesus   126
Prayer and power   126

False teachers condemned by
Jesus   127
Suffering triumphantly   127
The kingdom of God   127
Forgiveness and our response   127
The Son of man and the kingdom
of God   128
On the way to Jerusalem and
death   128
In the Jerusalem Temple among
enemies   128
Jesus in peril   129
Jesus on trial   129
The way of the cross   129
Jesus rises from death   129

Index   **130**

Acknowledgments   **133**

1 A man named Luke

What was Luke like?

In one sense nobody knows what Luke looked like, or even what he did. Was he tall and thin? Where was he born? Had he blue eyes or brown? Did he take after his mother or his father? Had he any brothers or sisters? Was he married with children? We simply don't know.

But we do know a great deal about him, things far more important than such facts. We know what he believed in. We know what he considered to be most important. And this is because we can read what he wrote.

Luke wrote two 'books', which he wanted people to read one after the other. The first is devoted to the life and teaching of Jesus. The second is about what happened to Jesus's followers after Jesus left them behind in this world. The first is known as the Gospel according to Luke. The second is called the Acts of the Apostles. Our book is about the first.

Reading people's minds

How can we know what anybody is really like? Look around your classroom and pick out for yourself two people. One of them may seem strong and tough, always the first to try and answer when the teacher asks a question, good at games, and always laughing. The other may be shy and reserved; working hard at lessons, and happiest either sitting in the library or doing chemistry experiments.

You might find out a bit more about them. For instance, that the first has parents who run a shop, and a younger brother who was killed in a road accident. And that the second has two sisters and a brother; a father who drives a railway train and a mother who works as a part-time teacher.

With all this information, do you really know these people — what they are like inside?

Suppose you discovered that the first writes poetry but doesn't show it to anyone for fear of being thought stupid. If you were allowed to read some of this poetry, you might realise that even though the younger brother was killed five years ago, he is still greatly missed, and that here is a someone who is really interested in writing poetry, but doesn't dare tell even the teacher about this secret ambition. Maybe all the laughter is a way of covering up an inner sadness.

The second person might secretly write spy stories — which could account for all the time spent in the library — and, although timid in class, might have the most amazing imaginary adventures that no one else dreams of, in exciting foreign lands.

If you could read the poems or the stories of these two, you would learn far more about the way they think than by just looking at them or knowing what their homes are like. In a similar way, we can read Luke's mind through reading his gospel.

Luke's hero

Who is the most famous person that ever lived? Amongst all the candidates different people could suggest, Jesus — a man who lived nearly two thousand years ago and was killed when he was scarcely more than thirty years old — is one who would come top of many lists. He was Luke's hero.

Throughout the world today millions of people try to follow his teachings and regard him as their saviour. And since his time on earth thousands of books have been written about his life.

His followers have accepted four of these as greater than any others. They are the first four books of the New Testament, the 'gospels' (as we call them all) of Matthew, Mark and John, as well as Luke.

Four portraits of Jesus

As with most portraits of the same man done by different people, each of the four gospels shows us a different face of Jesus. One of the gospel writers, John, at the end of his gospel wrote, 'There are many things which Jesus did. If every one of them were written down, I suppose that the world itself could not contain the books that could be written.' (John chapter 21, verse 25). Matthew, Mark, Luke and John chose what they wanted to write about from all that the earliest followers of Jesus told them. They chose sometimes the same stories about Jesus and sometimes different ones. Each one contains teachings by Jesus and memories of what happened to him which are not found in the other three gospels.

A 'gospel'

Gospel is an odd word to describe the story of someone's life. It really means 'good news'.

The good news, or gospel, of Jesus was that God's rule was coming

In Peking the unarmed demonstrate against violence.

*Jesus said, 'When a man hits you on the cheek, offer him the other cheek too.'
Say whether you think we can stop violence peacefully, as Jesus apparently
believed. Give your reasons, with reference to today's political events.*

over all the world. Jesus announced that the reign of God would in the end triumph.

Luke believed him, even though no one could be certain about this. As we shall see in Luke's gospel, Jesus warned his followers that earthly rulers would savagely persecute them and even kill them — as they were to kill him. Even so, Luke believed, they had to trust that in the end God would not let them down.

Good news for the downtrodden

That God was to take over the world is bad news for the evil men and women who wish to run it in their own interests. It is good news for those who are trodden on by such people, for Jesus believed that God stands for justice and love, not for cruelty and hatred. This was the God all the Jews had learned of from the writings of the prophets in the Jewish Bible, which Christians today call the Old Testament and which Jesus had studied and loved all his life.

The coming of God's rule, he believed, was tremendous news for anyone who was suffering in this world. More: as Luke shows us, Jesus believed that he himself had been born on earth to bring about God's rule. The good news, or gospel, was specially bound up with Jesus's own life and teaching.

Luke tells us that one day Jesus stood up in the synagogue (see page 6) at Nazareth, the town where he had been brought up, and read from the book of Isaiah:

> The Spirit of the Lord is upon me,
> because he has anointed me to preach good news to the poor.
> He has sent me to proclaim release to the captives
> and recovering of sight to the blind,
> to set at liberty those who are oppressed,
> to proclaim the acceptable year of the Lord.
>
> (Isaiah chapter 61, verses 1f)

Jesus added, 'Today this scripture has been fulfilled in your hearing.' (Luke chapter 4, verses 16 to 21)

In this passage God promises both healing for the sick and freedom for those unjustly imprisoned. These words thus still have political implications, about human rights for instance. On 10 December 1948 the United Nations adopted a 'Universal Declaration of Human Rights', which included the statement that every law-abiding person had a right to liberty.

Forty years later the BBC broadcast a TV programme called 'Human Rights — How Much Do We Care?' This was how the *Radio Times* announced it:

Prisoners of Conscience

'The soldiers poured petrol over me and then threw a lighted match.'

The words of a Chilean woman. Her offence? Walking on the street on the day of a national strike. 'I was beaten with an iron bar. I heard mothers tortured in front of their children.' The words of a Turkish student. His offence? Membership of a legal opposition party. Exactly 40 years ago today the United Nations adopted the Universal Declaration of Human Rights. Yet people are still locked away simply for speaking their minds.
(*Radio Times*, 10 December 1988)

Few believed Jesus

The passage Jesus chose to read in the synagogue was from the Jewish prophet Isaiah (chapter 61, verses 1f). In it Isaiah speaks of God's chosen servant, whom the Jews expected to come one day to declare that from then on the rule of evil men and women would be replaced by God's rule. Jesus was claiming to be that chosen servant.

Luke here is making a stupendous claim for Jesus, and using Jesus's own words to do so. Many people (as Luke himself tells us) refused to believe Jesus really was such good news. After all, they knew Jesus's parents. They had seen him grow up as a boy. How could he be God's special messenger, sent to bring about God's rule on earth?

Jesus's answer was to ask them to look again at their scriptures. Many of the prophets of the Old Testament had not been honoured among their own people. He pointed out that even the greatest figures of the Bible had been powerless where people had no faith in them. For this reason, Jesus said, he expected many of his own people to reject him.

His words made them extremely angry. They threw him out of the city, Luke records, leading him to the brow of the hill on which it stood, in order to throw him off it, but he escaped (chapter 4, verses 22 to 30).

Luke the passionate believer

Luke, like the other three gospel writers, did not share the view of the people of Nazareth. He believed that Jesus here spoke nothing but the truth about himself. Like Matthew, Mark and John, therefore, he is called an 'evangelist', that is the writer of a gospel (for evangelist comes from the Greek word for good news).

His main reason for writing is to reveal to other men and women that what Jesus said about himself was true. He wrote his gospel because he wanted others to share his own faith. And that is what all the evangelists did.

Can we trust Luke?

Luke wants above all to make people agree with him about Jesus. He wants to show that everything he believed about Jesus was grounded on what had actually happened.

So in the first four verses of his gospel he tells us precisely this. He is writing, he says, for a man named Theophilus, which means beloved of God. The man, we gather, is a high-up Roman official, for Luke calls him your excellency.

Theophilus already knows a lot about Jesus. Luke says that he now intends 'to write an orderly account for you . . . that you may know the truth concerning the things of which you have been informed'.

Luke also promises that his story will be historically accurate. He claims that what he writes comes from information handed down by eyewitnesses of what happened. These eyewitnesses were men and women who had first-hand knowledge of the life and teaching of Jesus.

He could also draw on earlier accounts of what had happened, for, he writes, even before he started to write his gospel 'many have undertaken to compile a narrative of the things which have been accomplished among us'.

These were his sources. He tells us about them because he wants us to trust him. Let's look at some of these sources.

Luke used Mark's gospel

Luke states that part of what he has to tell is based on earlier gospels. Apart from a few fragments, only one of these has survived, and that is the gospel of Mark.

For many years most people believed that of our four gospels the one by Mark could not have been written first. Since it is shorter than the other four, they assumed Mark had read maybe Matthew and cut his gospel down.

But when scholars began to look more closely at the matter, some felt that this could not be true. What they found was that wherever the stories of Mark appear in Matthew's gospel, it is Matthew who cuts them down. The same happens often when Luke borrows stories from Mark. And whenever all three — Matthew, Mark and Luke — tell the same story, Mark is nearly always not the shortest but the longest.

You can try and experiment to check this by reading three passages telling the same story; for example the story of how Jesus healed a leper, as told by Mark, Matthew and Luke.

How Jesus healed a leper

Mark chapter 1, verses 40 to 45

And a leper came to him beseeching him, and kneeling said to him, 'If you will, you can make me clean.' Moved with pity, he stretched out his hand and touched him, and said to him, 'I will; be clean.' And immediately the leprosy left him, and he was made clean. And he sternly charged him, and sent him away at once, and said to him, 'See that you say nothing to anyone; but go, show yourself to the priest, and offer for your cleansing what Moses commanded, for a proof to the people.' But he went out and began to talk freely about it, and to spread the news, so that Jesus could no longer openly enter a town, but was out in the country; and people came to him from every quarter.

Matthew chapter 8, verses 1 to 4

When he came down from the mountain, great crowds followed him; and behold, a leper came to him and knelt before him, saying, 'Lord, if you will, you can make me clean.' And he stretched out his hand and touched him, saying, 'I will; be clean.' And immediately his leprosy was cleansed. And Jesus said to him, 'See that you say nothing to any one; but go, show yourself to the priest, and offer the gift that Moses commanded, for a proof to the people.'

Luke chapter 5, verses 12 to 16

When he was in one of the cities, there came a man full of leprosy; and when he saw Jesus, he fell on his face and besought him, 'Lord, if you will, you can make me clean.' And he stretched out his hand, and touched him, saying, 'I will; be clean.' And immediately the leprosy left him. And he charged him to tell no one; but 'go and show yourself to the priest, and make an offering for your cleansing, as Moses commanded, for a proof to the people.' But so much the more the report went far abroad concerning him; and great multitudes gathered to hear and to be healed of their infirmities. But he withdrew to the wilderness and prayed.

Mark's is obviously by far the longest version. Luke, like Matthew, is copying Mark's stories and then shortening them.

Next, the scholars spotted that Mark is the one whose account again and again sets the pattern for the other two. They usually follow his order of the events of Jesus's life. From time to time they disagree with him. Sometime we can see them correcting his account, or changing it in various ways.

But both Luke and Matthew rely on Mark most of the time. When one of them changes Mark's version, the other does not. Try a second experiment to demonstrate this, by reading for instance the story of a fig tree as told by Mark (chapter 11, verses 12 to 14 and 20 to 25), Matthew (chapter 21, verses 18 to 22) and Luke (chapter 13, verses 6 to 9).

Obviously here Matthew copied and shortened Mark. Luke, on the other hand, decided that the story in Mark needed changing, and put in a parable instead. (For more on his fig tree see pages 11 to 12.)

Other gospels?

Of the 1,150 or so verses in Luke's gospel, some 320 come from Mark. Can we find another earlier gospel that he used as well?

None apparently exists. What we can do is discover where Luke and Matthew offer information about Jesus which is not found in Mark. Maybe that came from the same source — an earlier gospel which has been lost, or at least a collection of stories about the life and teaching of Jesus made by someone else.

There are in fact only around 250 such verses common to Luke and Matthew. This means that Luke did a great deal of his own research when writing his gospel. Almost half of it comes from him alone. Some of the finest stories Jesus ever told would have been lost if we did not have Luke's gospel.

The material Luke and Matthew have in common is thus not very much. It includes one miracle worked by Jesus, when he heals a Roman officer's servant. It includes information about Jesus's baptism which Mark does not tell us. The rest is new teaching by Jesus. (Matthew chapter 3, verse 13 to chapter 4, verse 11, and chapter 8, verses 5 to 13; Luke chapter 3, verses 21f, chapter 4, verses 1 to 13 and chapter 7, verses 1 to 10)

Some things Luke alone tells us

If Luke copied earlier stories about Jesus which we can read in other gospels, he also added marvellous material that we can find nowhere else.

Without the gospel of Luke we would know far less about Jesus's relationship with women. No other gospel tells the following tale, which displays Jesus's compassion for a widow:

> . . . he went into a city called Nain, and his disciples and a great crowd went with him. As he drew near to the gate of the city,

behold, a man who had died was being carried out, the only son of his mother, and she was a widow; and a large crowd from the city was with her. And when the Lord saw her, he had compassion on her, and said to her, 'Do not weep.' And he came and touched the bier, and the bearers stood still. And he said, 'Young man, I say to you, arise.' And the dead man sat up, and began to speak. And he gave him to his mother.

(chapter 7, verses 11 to 15)

We learn only from Luke of some women who used their own money to care for Jesus and his disciples. Without Luke's gospel we should hardly guess that Jesus's disciples included women at all.

This special material in Luke also contains some of his most striking parables: the Pharisee and the tax collector, the good Samaritan, the rich fool, Dives and Lazarus (pages 44–46, 66, 85); as well as some remarkable miracle stories: the raising of the widow's son which we have just read, the healing of a crippled woman and the healing of ten lepers.

Oral tradition

Where did Luke find all this extra information? Was there another gospel — now lost — which Luke copied when he was writing these parts of his own gospel? Perhaps. No one has ever found it.

What Luke himself tells us is that he asked eyewitnesses and those who preached about Jesus (chapter 1, verse 2). So these miracles and parables which he tells may not even have been written down before Luke's time. Do you know any older people in your community who love to tell stories? Maybe such a person is your own father or your own grandmother. If so, notice how they often lovingly repeat the tales. Each time they repeat them, the details remain the same.

We call this 'oral tradition'. Luke may easily have learned these special stories about Jesus from the lips of men and women he had met and talked to.

They contain aspects of Jesus which no other gospel reveals. Without Luke we would not know that Jesus deeply shocked a man who had the position of 'ruler of the synagogue' by curing a cripple on the 'sabbath', a day when no good Jew (such as Jesus was) was supposed to work. We would not know that Jesus annoyed many people by having a meal with a hated tax collector in the city of Jericho. Tax collectors were 'outcasts' and as we shall see (pages 52 to 57) Luke's gospel shows us a Jesus who especially wanted to bring outcasts back to God.

Changing the point

Oral tradition holds on to the facts of the tales that are being handed on.

But often too the stories are given a new twist. Take a film about the American Wild West. Cowboys will certainly feature, and often Red Indians. The story is basically the same, but sometimes the Red Indians are portrayed as totally wicked; at other times the baddies are the cowboys. The point of a story can be altered, even while what happens remains the same.

Luke has at least three sources:

Mark,

his common source with Matthew,

oral tradition.

The stories he takes from them and retells had been told and retold over a period of nearly fifty years, if we accept that Luke was written forty-five years after the death of Jesus, as most scholars say.

Luke tells us stories whose main points can easily have changed over these forty-five years.

An example: the withered fig tree

Sometimes we can see this change happening, when we compare what Luke wrote down with what his source Mark wrote on the same topic. Take the following story from Luke. It shows that at times Luke was

The pleasure of telling and listening to stories.

Write out one of the many stories told by Jesus as found in Luke's gospel. What are the main points of the story? Look at the same story in one of the other gospels. Has this been altered in any way?

willing to alter quite decisively what he had learned from Mark's gospel.

Mark tells us that as Jesus and his followers were approaching Jerusalem he saw a fig tree which should have been carrying a crop of figs. When he found there were no figs on it, he said, 'May no one ever eat fruit from you again.' The following morning they passed the fig tree again and Peter, one of his chief disciples, said, 'Master, look! The fig tree which you cursed has withered.' (Mark chapter 11, verses 12 to 14 and 20f)

Luke clearly does not like this story. Instead of retelling it, at this point he includes in his gospel a parable:

> And he told this parable: 'A man had a fig tree planted in his vineyard; and he came seeking fruit on it and found none. And he said to the vinedresser, "Lo, these three years I have come seeking fruit on this fig tree, and I find none. Cut it down; why should it use up the ground?" And he answered him, "Let it alone, sir, this year also, till I dig about it and put on manure. And if it bears fruit next year, well and good; but if not, you can cut it down."'

> (Luke chapter 13, verses 6 to 9)

Here there is no hint of cursing. What Luke is emphasising is forgiveness, and the possibility of being given a second chance — which is one of his favourite themes (see below, page 83).

When did Luke write his gospel?

Nobody really knows. It must have been some time in the first century of the Christian era, for we know people were using his gospel in the second century AD.

Also, Luke seems to have written his gospel some time after the destruction and fall of Jerusalem, which took place in AD 70. If you read Luke chapter 19, verses 41 to 44, and chapter 21, verses 20 and 24, you can see that although the words Jesus uses are *predicting* the fall of Jerusalem at the hands of the Romans, Luke has enriched them by adding descriptions of the actual event.

At the same time Luke's gospel was addressed to Christians who were not yet being viciously persecuted by the Romans. That had happened earlier under the emperor Nero; and it was to happen later in AD 95 at the time of the emperor Domitian.

A reasonable guess for the date of Luke's gospel, therefore, would be some time in the 80s or the early 90s of the first century AD.

Luke the careful historian

As we read through Luke's gospel we discover that he passionately wanted to tell his story with complete accuracy. He set out to be a totally trustworthy historian.

Sometimes this made him put into his story details which hardly seem to matter. He tells us, for example, that because 'a decree went out from Caesar Augustus that all the world should be enrolled' everybody had to go to his own city. This is why Mary, the mother of Jesus, even when she was pregnant, was taken by her husband Joseph from Nazareth where they lived to Joseph's own city, Bethlehem.

Luke thus explains why Jesus was born there and not in Nazareth. But he adds also, 'This was the first enrolment, when Quirinius was governor of Syria.' (chapter 2, verses 1 to 5)

There is no real reason why we need to know this. Luke puts it in because he wants to insist that everything he is telling us is the absolute historical truth. The story of Jesus is so remarkable that sometimes it seems scarcely believable. Luke is trying to show that even so it was no fairy tale but really happened. So he anchors it all in history.

He does exactly the same thing when he tells how John the Baptist began to preach to people in the wilderness and call them to be washed (or 'baptized') in the river Jordan. This section of his gospel begins by telling us that it all happened:

'Bethlehem' by Galambos Tamas.

In the fifteenth year of the reign of Tiberius Caesar, Pontius Pilate being governor of Judea, and Herod being tetrarch of Galilee, and

his brother Philip tetrarch of the region of Ituraea and Trachonitis, and Lysanias tetrarch of Abilene, in the high-priesthood of Annas and Caiaphas . . .

(chapter 3, verses 1f)

In one sense no one needs to know this. Yet for Luke it was important. He knew he had a remarkable story to tell. Though we now know he sometimes gets his facts wrong, he wants to demonstrate that everything he believes in really happened at a very clear time in history.

Essential information about Luke

What Paul tells us about Luke

For nearly two thousand years people have named the author of this gospel 'Luke'. Some ancient writers have given us more information about him. A historian called Eusebius says he came from a place called Antioch in Syria.

We can also do some detective work ourselves, using only the New Testament. The second book written by this man, the Acts of the Apostles, contains four passages where the author is clearly present, working with St Paul to spread the message of Jesus and sharing some of Paul's heroic and dangerous life. (These passages are Acts chapter 16, verses 10 to 17, chapter 20, verses 5 to 15, chapter 21, verses 1 to 18 and chapter 27, verse 1 to chapter 28, verse 16.)

Instead of writing that 'they' or 'he' or 'she' did something, in these passages the author of the Acts of the Apostles always uses the word 'we'. The author of the gospel and the Acts of the Apostles must, then, have been a companion of Paul. Perhaps Paul's preaching converted him. The evidence is that he was with Paul on his last journey to Rome.

Now in his own letters Paul three times mentions just such a man. His name was Luke. It seems perfectly likely that this Luke wrote both the gospel and the Acts of the Apostles.

Doctor Luke?

Once St Paul described this man as 'Luke the beloved physician' (Colossians 4, verse 14). Was he also a doctor?

His gospel itself gives us a hint that he was — and a doctor who was proud of his profession. At one point Luke tells us how a woman who could not stop bleeding was cured simply by touching the hem of Jesus's clothing. Now Mark's gospel tells the same story.

Mark adds that 'she had suffered much under many physicians, and had spent all that she had, and was no better but rather grew worse'.

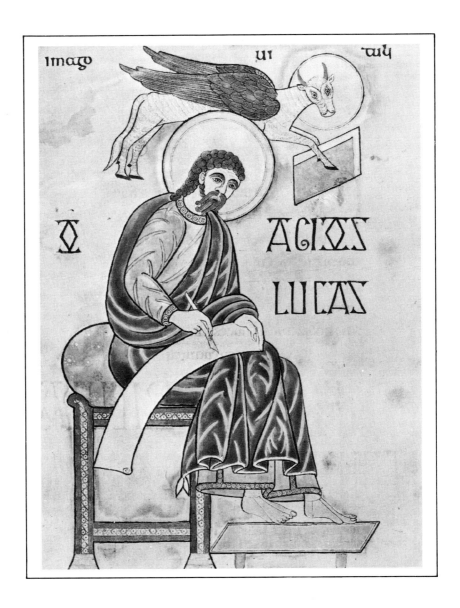

Luke.

This insult to the medical profession seems to have been too much for Luke, so he leaves it out altogether, simply commenting that the poor woman 'could not be healed by anyone'. (Luke chapter 8, verse 43, and Mark chapter 5, verse 26)

A non-Jew?

Those who are skilled at reading ancient languages tell us that Luke also wrote excellent Greek. Whenever he copied anything from Mark's gospel, we find him correcting or improving Mark's own Greek.

Obviously a well educated man (as any doctor would be), he could change his style of writing when he wished. Sometimes he wrote in the religious Greek used by those Jews who spoke Greek in their synagogues and in the Greek translation of the Jewish Bible. At other times he moved over to the everyday snappy Greek spoken by ordinary people of that time.

This has led many scholars to suppose that the man who wrote this gospel was not a Jew and would have been known to the Jews as a 'Gentile'. If this is so, Luke is certainly the only non-Jew to have written any book in the New Testament.

A Gentile's concerns

If Luke was a Gentile, we should expect his gospel to be concerned with parts of Jesus's teaching not found in the gospels of those whose chief concern was the Jewish world. This turns out to be true. Luke has two especial concerns not found to the same degree anywhere else in the New Testament. First, he is trying to show that Jesus came for the sake of everyone — not just for the Jews. Secondly, he wants to display, if he can, that Jesus (and all his followers) need not be enemies of the non-Jewish world.

The gospel is for everyone

Jesus hardly ever taught non-Jews, though he could praise the faith of — for example — Roman soldiers who came to beg his help or the decency of those who did their duty honestly. Because he spent nearly all of his working life trying to bring his message only to Jews, many of the early Christians thought that they could forget non-Jews (or 'Gentiles') altogether.

Theophilus

Luke made it clear very early on in his gospel that he was presenting a Jesus whose good news was for Gentiles too. The Theophilus to whom he addressed his gospel was as we have seen probably a high-ranking Roman. Luke tells us that Jesus had come as 'a light to open the eyes of the Gentiles' (chapter 2, verse 32). At the end of this gospel he portrays Jesus teaching his followers 'that repentance and forgiveness of sins should be preached in his name to all nations, beginning in Jerusalem' (chapter 24, verse 47).

Jesus's family tree

Both Luke and Matthew in their gospels give us what they claim is Jesus's family tree. Matthew traces it back as far as Abraham. For

Matthew this is enough: Abraham is the father of the Jewish nation, and Jesus is descended from this great man.

With Luke the family tree of Jesus is taken back past Abraham as far as Adam — traditionally the founder of all humankind. Luke wishes us to see that Jesus belongs not just to his own Jewish race but to all men and women. (Luke chapter 3, verses 23 to 38, and Matthew chapter 1, verses 1 to 17)

Seventy missionaries

An episode found in no other gospel emphasised Luke's desire to show that Jesus came to save the whole world. He appointed seventy (or seventy-two according to some versions) of his followers 'and sent them ahead of him, two by two, into every town and place where he himself was about to come' (chapter 10, verse 1). Luke's account here differs from Matthew's, where only twelve are sent out. Why?

The answer is that Matthew speaks of twelve because he is still thinking chiefly of Jewish converts to Jesus's teaching. The Jews from long ago had been divided up into twelve tribes. But the Jews also believed that the rest of the world consisted of seventy (or some said seventy-two) other nations. Luke is now extending the mission to the Jews to include the possibility that all the people of the world can accept Jesus as their leader.

Good Gentiles, ready to believe

Luke describes a miracle (which is also found in Matthew's gospel), when Jesus healed the dying slave of a Roman centurion. The centurion so much trusts Jesus that he does not even ask him to come to his house, where the slave is lying. He begs Jesus simply to say a word to cure the slave. Jesus does so, adding, 'I tell you, not even in Israel have I found such faith.'

In this story Luke introduces a fascinating element not found in Matthew. The centurion, instead of approaching Jesus himself, asks some leading Jews to do so for him. They tell Jesus what a good man he is, saying, 'He is worthy to have you do this for him, for he loves our nation, and has built for us our synagogue.' (chapter 7, verses 1 to 10; compare this with Matthew chapter 8, verses 5 to 10)

Christians are good citizens

Just as Luke describes this officer of the Roman army who is good to Jews, so he also wants to show that Christians can be good citizens of the Roman empire. This was not an easy task, since Jesus had been executed under the authority of the Roman ruler of Judea, Pontius Pilate.

In addition, Christians had already suffered persecution at the hands of the Romans. When a fire in Rome destroyed half the city in AD 64, the emperor Nero blamed the Christians for starting it. Countless innocent Christians were savagely put to death.

The Romans found Jesus innocent

When he comes to describe Jesus's trial, Luke asserts that his Roman judge Pilate declared Jesus innocent no fewer than three times. Luke goes further, insisting that another Roman ruler, Herod Antipas, also found that Jesus was not an enemy of the state. Pilate, says Luke, 'called together the chief priests and the rulers and the people, and said to them, "You brought me this man as one who was perverting the people; and after examining him before you, I did not find this man guilty of your charges against him; neither did Herod, for he sent him back to us. Behold, nothing deserving death has been done by him; I will therefore chastise him and release him.'

Luke then says that Pilate's audience 'all cried out together, "Away with this man."' In short, he sets out to show that Jesus's enemies amongst his own people, not the Romans, were responsible for his execution on a cross. (chapter 23, verses 13 to 18)

The parable of the coin and the tribute money

Jesus's enemies had accused him before Pilate of 'perverting our nation, and forbidding us to give tribute to Caesar' (chapter 23, verse 2).

Luke had already dealt with this accusation by telling how these same people had sent to Jesus spies who pretended to be sincere but were really wanting to trick him into making some remarks attacking the rule of the Romans. They asked him, 'Is it lawful for us to give tribute [i.e. taxes] to Caesar or not?'

Many Jews at this time would have been deeply upset if Jesus had answered 'yes', since they deeply hated Roman rule. If he had answered 'no' he would have immediately been branded as a rebel by the Roman authorities. Jesus, says Luke, perceived their craftiness in asking the question. This is how he answered them.

'Show me a coin,' he said. Then he asked, 'Whose likeness and superscription has it?' They answered, 'Caesar's.' Jesus then said, 'Render to Caesar the things that are Caesar's, and to God the things that are God's.'

As Luke comments, 'they were not able in the presence of the people to catch him by what he said; but marvelling at his answer they were silent.' Jesus's enemies had failed to make him out as a traitor to Rome. So, Luke wants to say, neither are Jesus's followers disloyal members of the Roman empire. (chapter 20, verses 19 to 26)

The Roman soldier at the crucifixion

Immediately after describing Jesus's death on the cross, Luke tells us that the Roman centurion on guard there praised God and said, 'Certainly this man was innocent!'

We can be almost sure that Luke was here altering what he had learned from others. Both Matthew's gospel and Mark's gospel tell us that the soldier cried, 'Truly this man was the Son of God!' (Luke chapter 23, verse 47; Matthew chapter 27, verse 54; Mark chapter 15, verse 39)

For Luke it seemed at this point more important for a Roman officer to declare Jesus innocent than to confess his faith that Jesus was the Son of God.

Assignments

K U   1   Write down what you know about Luke.

K U   2   Give the names of the two books written by Luke and say what each was about.

U E   3   Why are the first four books of the New Testament so important to us?

U   4   What is the meaning of the word 'gospel'?

E   5   Why did many people find it difficult to believe that Jesus was God's chosen servant?

U   6   What do you understand by the word 'Evangelist'?

E   7   'He has sent me to proclaim release to the captives and recovery of sight to the blind, to set at liberty those who are oppressed, to proclaim the acceptable year of the Lord.'

     What are the political implications of these words today? Use your library and newspapers, and then discuss your findings in groups.

     8   Read the following passage:

     And he told this parable: 'A man had a fig tree planted in his vineyard; and he came seeking fruit on it and found none. And he said to the vinedresser, "Lo, these three years I have come seeking fruit on this fig tree, and I find none. Cut it down; why should it use up the ground?" And he answered him, "Let it alone, sir, this year also, till I dig about it and put on manure. And if it bears fruit next year, well and good; but if not, you can cut it down."'

(Luke chapter 13, verses 6 to 9)

U   (a) What is the point of this parable?
K U   (b) Compare it with Mark's account of an unfruitful fig tree (chapter 11, verses 12–14, 20f).
U   (c) What does it tell us about Luke?

K　9　When do you think Luke wrote his gospel? Give reasons for your answer.

K U　10　When Luke was writing his gospel he drew on earlier accounts of what had happened. What sources did he use, and what do we learn about Luke from this?

K E　11　Luke tells some stories that are not found in any other gospel. Write about two of them and state why you think they are important today.

U E　12　What do you understand by the words 'oral tradition'? Do you think we can rely on such stories?

K U　13　Take two stories — one from Luke's gospel and one from Mark's gospel — and show how they differ. Why do you think Luke (or his sources) changed these stories?

U　14　How do we know that Luke and Paul were friends? What implications does this have?

K U　15　Pretend you are a person living in the time of Luke. You have just met him. Write a letter to a friend describing your meeting.

Key to the symbols alongside the assignments at the end of each chapter:

K　Knowledge
U　Understanding
E　Evaluation

2 The coming of the Son of God

The angel Gabriel brings a message to Mary

Luke tells us that Jesus's mother, Mary, was promised in marriage to a man named Joseph. Joseph, he says, was descended from the Jew's greatest king, David. Joseph and Mary lived at a place called Nazareth.

One day God's messenger (or 'angel') appeared before Mary. He is named as Gabriel — according to Jewish beliefs at that time, one of the seven greatest of the angels. Clearly he brings an extremely important message.

Gabriel said to Mary:

Hail, O favoured one, the Lord is with you.

At this Mary became anxious. What could the angel mean? Gabriel went on:

Do not be afraid, Mary, for you have found favour with God. And behold, you will conceive in your womb and bear a son, and you shall call his name Jesus.

What does 'Jesus' mean?

Jesus is a Greek name, a translation of the Jewish name Joshua, which means 'the Lord is salvation'. But now Gabriel spoke in verse, telling Mary that her son would be remarkable:

he would be called 'the Son of the Most High', that is, Son of God;
God would give him the throne of David;
he would reign over the Jewish race for ever;
his kingdom would never end.

Mary remained puzzled, for, as she told the angel, she was not yet married. She had never had sexual intercourse. The angel then said that she would bear a son, even though she remained a virgin. These are his words:

> The Holy Spirit will come upon you,
> and the power of the Most High will overshadow you;
> therefore the child to be born will be called holy,
> the Son of God.

At this Mary replied, 'Behold, I am the handmaid of the Lord; let it be to me according to your word.' (chapter 1, verses 26 to 38)

Son of God

In spite of being described as the Son of God at his birth, Jesus as Luke presents him to us seems remarkably reluctant to use the title of himself. At his trial his enemies ask, 'Are you the Son of God, then?' He replies not 'Yes', but 'You say that I am'.

Here we have to understand that he is defending himself against the charge that he is insulting God by claiming to be his Son. Yet elsewhere in the gospel as Luke tells it, he does not claim the title either.

What we find is that others point out who he is. Almost always they are supernatural beings, such as the angel who appears to Mary. The devil, tempting Jesus, mocks him by suggesting that he is perhaps not the Son of God (chapter 4, verses 3, 9); and unclean demons recognise him as the Son of God (chapter 4, verse 41, and chapter 8, verses 28f).

Twice Luke tells us that the voice of God himself declared Jesus to be his Son. The first was when Jesus was baptised. The second time occurred when he was transfigured.

The baptism of Jesus

Luke tells us that Jesus was about thirty years old when he began his ministry.

He had a relative named John, the son of Elizabeth (see page 26–27). John had begun to urge people to turn away from wickedness. Soon, he said, God's kingdom would come on earth. It would be set up by God's chosen servant. Luke quotes some words from the Old Testament prophet Isaiah (chapter 40) to describe what John was doing. Isaiah wrote:

> In the wilderness prepare the way of the Lord,
> make straight in the desert a highway for our God.

John clearly expected the coming of God's chosen servant to bring about God's rule on earth. To show that they had given up their evil ways and were now clean, John demanded that people should be dipped (baptised) in the river Jordan.

Jesus decided to join those who were being baptised. Luke describes John's preaching and activities, and then writes:

> Now when all the people were baptized, and when Jesus also had been baptized and was praying, the heaven was opened, and the Holy Spirit descended upon him in bodily form, as a dove, and a voice came from heaven, 'Thou art my beloved Son; with thee I am well pleased.'
>
> (chapter 3, verses 21f)

This heavenly blessing of Jesus, taken together with the quotation from Isaiah, presents Jesus as a turning point in divine and human history. All the past hopes of the Jewish people — who in the Bible are themselves sometimes called God's son — now cluster round Jesus; and he too is presented as humankind's hope for the future. He will bring God's rule upon earth, for he is the Son of God and his father is delighted with him.

The transfiguration of Jesus

Mount Moses.

Later in his ministry Jesus took three of his closest followers, Peter, James and John, to a mountain to pray. While he was praying, his appearance changed. His clothing became dazzlingly white. His followers saw two men talking with him. They were Moses — who had handed on to the Jews the law of God — and Elijah, one of the greatest

of the Jewish prophets. Here again Jesus is represented as being the heir of all the great jewels of Jewish religious life. Even the fact that they are on a mountain is important, for it was on Mount Sinai that Moses was privileged to receive the great commandments from God himself.

Jesus's followers are naturally afraid. They become even more frightened when they hear Jesus and his two companions speaking of his coming death. (Only Luke of all the gospel writers tells us this.)

Jesus is to leave the world. He calls this an 'exodus'. Just as at the 'exodus' long ago Moses led the Jews from captivity in Egypt, now Jesus is somehow to lead people to freedom by dying for them. Once again Luke is presenting Jesus as summing up all the past history of his nation and offering hope for everyone by his actions in the future.

Finally they hear a voice from heaven: 'This is my Son, my chosen; listen to him.' Jesus is confirmed as the Son of God with a unique mission to fulfil all that has happened in the past and to bring new life to the world. (chapter 9, verses 28 to 36)

'Son of God' and 'Son of man'

As we shall see as we read more of Luke's gospel, Jesus preferred to call himself 'Son of man' rather than 'Son of God'.

This seems to us an odd way of talking. A 'son of man' is, we suppose, simply a man. The Jews of Jesus's time did not see it like this. They remembered something written in the book of Daniel. The prophet has a vision of four beasts who represent the kingdoms of the world. Each one has its kingdom taken away and one is slain. Then, Daniel continues:

> behold, with the clouds of heaven
>   there came one like a son of man . . .
> And to him was given dominion
>   and glory and kingdom,
> that all peoples, nations and languages
>   should serve him;
> his dominion is an everlasting dominion,
>   which shall not pass away,
> and his kingdom one
>   that shall not be destroyed.
>
> (Daniel chapter 7, verses 13f)

Jesus himself is claiming, as the human face of God, to rule over the world for ever.

At the same time Luke shows him, even as a boy, accepting that God is his father in a special way. Jewish law laid down that every adult male should visit Jerusalem three times a year. When Jesus was twelve Mary and Joseph took him with them to the feast of the Passover (see pages 109–110).

Many people made this journey, and the young people stuck together. When Mary and Joseph set off home, they supposed Jesus was still with the other young people. They were wrong. They had left him behind.

After three days they began to worry about him. Returning to the Jerusalem Temple they found him there, sitting with the teachers, who were amazed at his understanding.

Mary asked her son how he could have treated them in this way, causing them such anxiety. He replied, 'How is it that you sought me? Did you not know that I must be in my Father's house?'

Again Mary is said to have kept all this in her heart. And Jesus obediently went home with them, where, Luke observes, he 'increased in wisdom and in stature, and in favour with God and man'. He remains a responsible son, in spite of his unique destiny. (chapter 2, verses 41 to 52)

The virgin birth

In fact, Luke's gospel denies that Jesus was a natural son of a human male. We know that, normally, for a virgin to bear a child is impossible. Without a sexual relationship between the parents, children are not born. The statement that Jesus was born in such a miraculous way is found only in Luke's gospel and Matthew's gospel. Matthew and Luke are insisting here that there is some special relationship between God and Jesus which applies to no other human being. Jesus was conceived not by normal human sexual intercourse but through 'the power of the Most High' and by 'the Holy Spirit' coming upon Mary.

One oddity about Luke and Matthew is that later in their gospels they are both capable of describing Joseph as Jesus's father. Both of them, for instance, trace Jesus's family tree back not through Mary but through Joseph. In fact in Jewish law once Joseph and Mary had married, Jesus would be accepted as Joseph's son.

Luke also spotted the problem, for at the beginning of his list of Jesus's ancestors he writes not that he was Joseph's son but that he was 'the son (as was supposed) of Joseph (chapter 3, verse 23). Luke was not stupid enough to contradict himself so foolishly.

Mary visits Elizabeth

Gabriel told Mary that her relative, Elizabeth, was pregnant. Mary decided to visit her instantly. Another remarkable event occurred. As soon as she entered Elizabeth's home, the unborn baby leaped in

Elizabeth's womb, as though he recognised already that Mary's child would be greater than he.

Inspired by God's spirit, Elizabeth too showed the same insight. She cried out, 'Blessed are you among women, and blessed is the fruit of your womb! And why is this granted to me that the mother of my Lord should come to me?'

Now it was Mary's turn to rejoice, in words which we now call 'the Magnificat' (a name taken from the Latin translation of its first word). First she declares her great gratitude that God had blessed her — his handmaiden, or slave — in this way.

The second part of the Magnificat speaks of the gratitude of all who need his help:

> He has showed strength with his arm,
> he has scattered the proud in the imagination of their hearts,
> he has put down the mighty from their thrones,
> and exalted those of low degree;
> he has filled the hungry with good things,
> and the rich he has sent empty away.

This is a very revolutionary song, coming from the lips of a humble woman long ago. Just as, Mary sang, God had 'done great things' for someone of such a 'low estate' as herself, so through her son Jesus he was going to do yet greater things for the lowly of this world. As for 'the proud', 'the mighty' and 'the rich' of this world, God through Jesus has declared himself their enemy and will through Jesus put them down. (chapter 1, verses 39 to 56)

Bethlehem

According to Luke, Jesus was born not in Nazareth, where his parents lived, but in Bethlehem. Was this really so?

Some people have doubted it, for two reasons. First, they say, Luke and his fellow-Christians would want to say he was born there because Bethlehem was known as the city of King David, since David himself had been born there around a thousand years earlier. Secondly, they point out, one of the Jewish prophets (Micah) had declared that out of Bethlehem would come the future ruler. So Christians, believing that Jesus was David's true successor, felt that he ought to have been born in David's city.

As a good historian, Luke looked round to find a reason why Joseph and his pregnant bride-to-be Mary would have left Nazareth and gone to Bethlehem. This is his answer:

> In those days a decree went out from Caesar Augustus that all the
> world should be enrolled. This was the first enrolment, when

Quirinius was governor of Syria. And all went to be enrolled, each to his own city. And Joseph also went up from Galilee, from the city of Nazareth, to Judea, to the city of David, which is called Bethlehem, because he was of the house and lineage of David, to be enrolled with Mary, his betrothed, who was with child.

(chapter 2, verses 1 to 5)

Unfortunately Luke's facts are not quite right. So far as we know the whole Roman empire never had a universal census. Ten years or so after Jesus's birth there was a census of Palestine, his homeland, during Quirinius's years as governor.

But Luke could be nearly right. Before becoming governor, Quirinius had been a viceroy of the region. At that time enrolments were held every fourteen years in most parts of the Roman empire. Using this information scholars have worked out that there could have been such an enrolment in Palestine in 8 BC. Was that, then, the time when Jesus was born? If so, Mary and Joseph would have been obliged to make the eighty mile journey from Nazareth to Bethlehem, and there Jesus could have been born.

Jesus is born in a stable

For such a census the city would be bursting at its seams with visitors. *Bethlehem today.* When Joseph and Mary arrived there, they could not find lodgings. So

Jesus was born where the animals were fed, and his mother wrapped him in 'swaddling cloths', that is to say strips of cloth.

There is a deeper meaning to this birth in a stable. At the very start of his life Jesus is seen as one of the poor, belonging not with those who have huge possessions but counted as an outcast. Luke's gospel goes on to show him constantly on the side of the outcasts, the poor and the homeless. (chapter 2, verses 6f)

The homeless have not disappeared from the world since his day. In the second half of the twentieth century a charity named Shelter is still campaigning for those who cannot find decent homes in Britain. And even today a group of people concerned about homeless young people (the charity SPACE) feels the need to placard the walls of London with posters such as the one below.

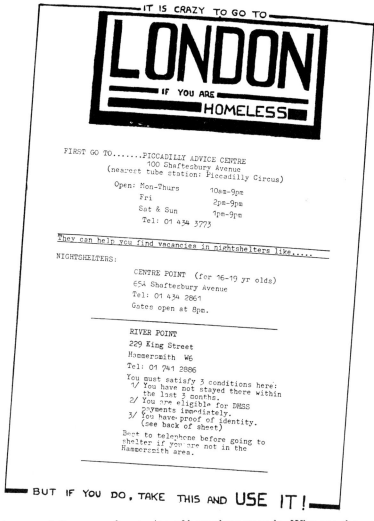

Look in your daily paper for stories of homeless people. Why are they homeless? What should be done for them?

An angel tells shepherds about the birth of Jesus

Poor and outcast people were the first to learn about the newly born Jesus. Shepherds today are respected members of many societies, but in Palestine in those days many religious people despised them. This was chiefly because their job made it impossible for them to obey every Jewish law.

Out in the fields, they were, for example, frequently unable to observe the rules about washing before eating. Also, the laws of Moses

No roof for their heads.

forbade any kind of work on the seventh day. Shepherds obviously could not neglect their flocks to obey this law.

Now, Luke says, an angel of God appeared to some shepherds who were that night watching over their flocks. A great light ('God's glory', Luke calls it) shone around them. The shepherds were scared, till the angel said he brought them good news of a great joy which everyone could share in. 'To you is born this day in the city of David a Saviour, who is Christ the Lord,' the angel continued. 'And this will be a sign for you: you will find a babe wrapped in swaddling cloths and lying in a manger.'

Suddenly a huge crowd of heavenly beings appeared with the angel, praising God and saying, 'Glory to God in the highest, and on earth peace among men with whom he is pleased.' (chapter 2, verses 8 to 14)

The shepherds worship Jesus

A shepherd with his flock in the fields near Bethlehem.

When the heavenly beings had left, the shepherds decided to go and worship the child in Bethlehem. There they found Mary, Joseph and the baby (who was still lying in the manger, a feeding trough for cattle). They told Mary and Joseph all that had happened, and, says Luke, 'Mary kept all these things, pondering them in her heart.'

Christmas

Each year most Christians specially remember these events at Christmas, on 25 December. One of their Christmas hymns sung on that day declares that Jesus was 'born this happy morning'.

In fact no one knows on what day Jesus really was born. It was only in the fourth century that Pope Julius I chose 25 December as the day of Jesus's birth. The day falls around the darkest days of the year, and the pope was probably trying to arrange a Christian festival to oppose pagans who celebrated the return of the sun with their own feasts at this time. These pagans used holly branches as wands for driving away evil spirits. Christians took them over and wove them into Christmas wreaths.

They also adopted the Roman custom of giving each other presents at this time. A hundred years ago the custom grew up in the West of hanging these on fir trees. Christmas, designed to celebrate the birth of a poor child who did not even have a proper cradle, has become a time of feasting and lavish spending.

The two faces of Christmas

The average British family spends about £300 on Christmas, according to a Woolworth survey of 1985. In that year the *Observer* newspaper published side by side two photographs, captioned, 'The two faces of Christmas'. One was captioned, 'Poverty in Bradford', the other, 'Shoppers queuing for cash in London's Regent Street'. The article declared:

The average British family spends about £300 on Christmas each year, according to a Woolworth survey. Woolworth's make their profit for the year in the three weeks leading up to Christmas so they should know.

Traditionally, Christmas is a time for thinking of others, so how much of this spending goes on charity? And how do families allocate their Christmas charity spending?

There are 153,710 registered charities in Britain alone and the scale of suffering among the countless starving and homeless in other parts of the world seems like a limitless hole down which any amount of money could be poured without altering the basic situation.

(*Observer*, 22 December 1985)

The angel's names for Jesus

As we have just seen, the angel called Jesus not by his own name but instead gave him three titles: Saviour, Christ and Lord. The meaning of these three names was clear to Luke but is not so clear to us today.

Saviour

This word is the closest of the three to Jesus's proper name, which we already know means 'the Lord is salvation'. But it has a deeper meaning too.

Saviour, in the Old Testament and in much other Jewish literature, almost always refers to God. God is often appealed to by people in trouble, in the confidence that he will save them. One of the Old Testament psalms begins:

> For God alone my soul waits in silence;
> from him comes my salvation.
> He only is my rock and my salvation,
> my fortress.
>
> (Psalm 62, verses 1f)

God was seen as saving men and women not just from danger but also from illness and mental torment.

Sometimes too the Bible described great men as saviours, if they had in some powerful way saved the Jewish people from disaster. Moses was the first to bear this name. But the angel here is definitely applying the word to Jesus not because he is in many respects like Moses but because he is in some special way related to God.

Like God he will save people, again not simply from danger but also from sickness and distress. Other New Testament books see Jesus as the one who can also save us from our sins and from death. He is, says one letter, 'our Saviour Christ Jesus, who abolished death'. Another declares that our great God and Saviour Jesus Christ 'gave himself for us to redeem us from all iniquity.' (2 Timothy chapter 1, verse 10 and Titus chapter 2 verses 13f)

Later in the gospel Luke will show Jesus doing precisely these things. A man named Jairus begs him to save his dying daughter. On the way to Jairus's house, a messenger arrives and says that the girl is already dead. Yet Jesus continues to Jairus's home and takes her by the hand calling, 'Child, arise.' Luke tells us that 'her spirit returned, and she got up at once; and he directed that something should be given her to eat'. (chapter 8, verses 40 to 42 and 49 to 56)

Another time some men brought a paralysed man, hoping that Jesus would heal him. Jesus was in a house so crowded that the only way they could get the man to him was by taking some tiles off the roof and letting him down on a bed. 'When Jesus saw their faith, he said, "Man, your sins are forgiven you."' Some of his enemies grew agitated. They asked, 'Who can forgive sins but God only?' This was precisely the point. Jesus himself was claiming on earth to have the same authority as God to forgive people's sins. (chapter 5, verses 17 to 26)

This aspect of Jesus's role as Saviour was extremely important for Luke, as we find if we read his second book, the Acts of the Apostles. Luke wrote that after Jesus had been killed, God raised him to his right hand 'as Leader and Saviour to give repentance to Israel and forgiveness of sins'. (Acts of the Apostles chapter 5, verse 31)

Christ

The word 'Christ' today is often used simply as if it were the surname of Jesus. It is in fact the Greek word for the Jewish word 'Messiah', and the Messiah was God's chosen one who would come and rule for ever.

'Messiah' did not always mean this. Originally it meant a person anointed with oil as a sign of being set apart for a special task. Jewish kings were anointed in this way, as were Jewish priests. Of all these men, the greatest in the eyes of the Jews was King David. One of their saddest texts declares that God promised David that his kingdom would last for ever (2 Samuel chapter 7, verses 12f). This had not happened. Soon the Jews were subject to other more powerful nations — at the time of Jesus, the Romans.

Over the years the Jews had worked out a new meaning to this promise. Many of them came to believe that one day to be looked forward to in the future, David, God's anointed or Messiah, would return to re-establish his kingdom. The prophet Jeremiah, for instance, promises that one day God will free his people from all those who dominate them and from strangers who make them their servants. Instead these people 'shall serve the Lord their God and David their king, whom I will raise up for them'. (Jeremiah chapter 30, verses 8f)

All this makes it clearer why it seemed so important to insist not only that Jesus was descended from King David but also that he was actually born in the city of David himself. Now the angel tells the shepherds that Jesus himself is the Christ, the anointed one so long expected by God's people.

Of course few believed it. Luke indicates that at first only what he calls 'demons' recognised who Jesus really was. Demons in those days were imagined as supernatural, evil beings who made people ill. When Jesus cured such sick people it was supposed that this was because he was stronger than the demons. These demons for their part spotted that in him the Christ had come.

'When the sun was setting, all those who had any that were sick with various diseases brought them to him; and he laid his hands on every one of them and healed them,' Luke tells us. 'And demons also came out of many, crying, "You are the Son of God!" But he rebuked them, and would not allow them to speak, because they knew that he was the Christ.' (chapter 4, verses 40f)

Why did Jesus not want people to be told that he was the Christ? One explanation is that his idea of what the Christ would do was quite different from the usual views. Many saw the coming Messiah as a political king, who would crush his enemies by force and then set up an earthly kingdom.

Jesus believed something utterly different. He held the astonishing notion that his destiny was to suffer, not to destroy others. He made this absolutely clear when one of his leading followers, Peter, declared his belief that Jesus was the Christ.

This marks a major turning point in Luke's gospel. Jesus had asked his closest followers, 'Who do the people say that I am?' He then asked, 'Who do you say that I am?'

Peter answered, 'The Christ of God.' Luke says that Jesus instantly 'charged and commanded them to tell this to no one, saying, "The Son of Man must suffer many things, and be rejected by the elders and chief priests and scribes, and be killed, and on the third day be raised."' (chapter 9, verses 18 to 22)

Lord

Jews so reverenced God that soon many of them refused even to speak his name. Instead they called him 'Lord', especially when they were praying.

They still regarded God, whether known as Lord or by his own name, as supremely great. Here is part of Psalm 24:

> Lift up your heads, O gates!
>   and be lifted up, O ancient doors!
>   that the King of glory may come in.
> Who is the King of glory?
>   The Lord, strong and mighty,
>   the Lord, mighty in battle!
> Lift up your heads, O gates!
>   and be lifted up, O ancient doors!
>   that the King of glory may come in.
> Who is this King of glory?
>   The Lord of hosts,
>   he is the King of glory!

(verses 7 to 10)

We have already seen Mary, as a devout Jew, declare her gratitude to God while calling him Lord. Now her son is called by the same name. Once again Jesus is seen as being in some way also God.

Jesus had a stern warning for people who called him Lord without truly meaning it, Luke reveals. 'Why do you call me "Lord, Lord," and not do what I tell you?' Jesus asked. 'Everyone who comes to me and hears my words and does them, I will show you what he is like: he is like a man building a house, who dug deep, and laid the foundation upon rock; and when a flood arose, the stream broke against that house, and could not shake it, because it had been well built. But he who hears and does not do them is like a man who built a house on the ground without a foundation; against which the stream broke, and immediately it fell, and the ruin of that house was great.' (chapter 6, verses 46 to 49)

Parents bring their children to be baptised. ▶

Assignments

U 1 What do you understand by the words 'son' and 'Son of God'? Comment on the two meanings.

E 2 Why do you think so many people find it difficult to believe in the virgin birth of Jesus? Do you think the virgin birth is an essential part of Christianity?

U 3 Try to compose a hymn or a poem about the birth of Jesus.

U E 4 What is the meaning of baptism? Do you think that baptism is as important today as it was in the time of Jesus?

E   5   Do you think it important to understand the Old Testament in order to understand the New? Illustrate your answer by referring to Luke's gospel.

U   6   Jesus preferred to call himself 'Son of man' rather than 'Son of God'. Give an explanation for this.

U E   7   Luke tells of the visit of Mary to Elizabeth. What do you find interesting about this account?

K   8   Mary sang 'the Magnificat'. What is this about?

U   9   What do you think is the significance of Jesus being born in a stable? In groups, discuss the problems of the homeless and say how you would try to resolve their problems.

E   10   'This house believes that Christmas has no meaning in the world today.' Write a speech supporting this motion.

U   11   Give the meanings of the following: Saviour; Christ; Lord.

K   12   Divide into groups and write a Nativity play.

E   13   Luke tells us that Mary delivered her first-born son, wrapped him in swaddling clothes and laid him in a manger. Do you think this has any significance today?

U E   14   John the Baptist made his preparation for his public ministry in the wilderness. Why do you think he did this? Do you think retreating into a wilderness is a sound idea?

U   15   Why do you think it was important to insist that Jesus was not only descended from King David but that he was also born in the city of King David himself?

E   16   The aspect of Jesus's role as Saviour was extremely important to Luke. Can you say why and support your answer with quotations from the Bible?

U   17   Discuss why Jesus did not want people to be told that he was the Christ.

3 Luke's Jesus

Looking at people through different eyes

Think of a woman in her fifties. She can be many different things to different people. Within her own family she may be both a mother and a grandmother. As her grandchildren grow up they will see quite different sides of her character from those seen by her children.

She may have been a strong parent, determined to keep her children under control at the same time as loving them. With her grandchildren she becomes a very different woman: she is soft, letting them have too much of their own way, always bringing presents, spoiling them.

As for her husband, he probably sees her as someone different again — a friend and companion, someone he can always rely on, someone who looks after him when he is ill or low, someone he has to care for in his turn. And if either of her parents are still alive, they will almost certainly still see her as their child, and therefore as in some ways still a child, even though she is a mature woman over fifty years old.

Then she goes out to work. By now she has risen to be, say, a bank manager. Her fellow-managers look upon her as an entertaining colleague, always ready for a joke, supporting them whenever they need help. Her juniors, on the other hand, look on her as the boss, even something of a stern, remote person. As for the bank's customers, to some she seems entirely helpful, sympathetic and ready to help out with a loan where necessary. To others whose accounts are never properly in order she seems like a dragon.

Yet she is one and the same person. People simply view her differently. Perhaps all their viewpoints are needed if we are to get close to knowing her. And still we can only guess what she thinks about herself.

The gospel writers' views

Jesus, too, was a different person to the different people who met him. Some adored him; some feared him; some followed him to death; some

Here is a modern artist's view of Jesus: 'Christ in the wilderness' by Stanley Spencer.

What do you think is going through his mind as he gazes at the Scorpion?

followed from afar; some hated him so much that they killed him. What was he really like? Who was he? What did he think about himself? As we read the four gospels we see four versions of the same man.

Of course all four gospels deal with the same person, Jesus of Nazareth. Often they tell the same stories about him or repeat his teaching in virtually the same words. Yet because they were written by four quite different people, each one gives us a different view of him. There is nothing surprising about this. As we have just shown, it is something that happens with everybody.

Luke's own picture of Jesus

What is special about Luke's Jesus? The following are some aspects of Jesus which Luke shows, and which we do not see in the portraits painted by the other three gospel writers?

Jesus's love for the poor and lowly

Luke continually stresses Jesus's sympathy for the poor and lowly. It is a love which those closest to him also share. His mother Mary, for instance, in Luke's account, shows that even before he was born she understood that her son would care for the poor and the underdog. As soon as she knew she would give birth to him, she sang that God had:

> ... shown strength with his arm,
> he has scattered the proud in the imagination of their hearts,
> he has put down the mighty from their thrones,
> and exalted those of low degree;
> he has filled the hungry with good things.
>
> (chapter 1, verses 51 to 53)

Later, John the Baptist, Jesus's cousin, teaches that the Jews must be generous: 'He who has two coats, let him share with him who has none; and he who has food, let him to likewise.' (chapter 3, verse 11)

As we have already seen (page 5), Jesus takes on himself Isaiah's prophecy that God's messenger shall 'preach good news to the poor'. The poor, he says, even though suffering in this world, will be given the kingdom of God, and those who go hungry today will be satisfied. (chapter 6, verses 20f)

So he urged people to love and help the poor, and in fact all those in need. 'When you give a dinner or a banquet,' he said, 'do not invite your brothers or your kinsmen or rich neighbours, lest they also invite you in return, and you be repaid. But when you give a feast, invite the poor, the maimed, the lame, the blind, and you will be blessed, because they cannot repay you. You will be repaid at the resurrection of the just.' (chapter 14, verses 12 to 14)

Luke also repeats the story in Mark's gospel of how a rich man came to Jesus and asked, 'Good Teacher, what shall I do to inherit eternal life?' Jesus told him to keep the commandments laid down by God in the Bible:

Do not commit adultery,
Do not kill,
Do not steal,
Do not bear false witness,
Honour your father and mother.

When the man replied, 'All these I have observed from my youth,' Jesus answered, 'One thing you still lack. Sell all that you have and distribute to the poor, and you will have treasure in heaven; and come, follow me.' (chapter 18, verses 18 to 22)

Riches do not always bring happiness in this world. When Christina Onassis died in November 1988, this is what an English newspaper wrote about her:

CHRISTINA ONASSIS was a classic example of the old saw 'money can't buy happiness'.

Her shipping fortune was reputed to be worth £350 million, but her personal life was marred by grief and unhappiness. She had lost both her parents and her beloved only brother by the time she was 24 and she married and separated from four husbands.

(*Independent*, 21 November 1988)

Jesus's attitude to the rich

If the poor are to be filled, as Mary's song declares, the rich will be sent away empty. 'Woe to you that are rich, for you have received your consolation,' Jesus says. 'Woe to you that are full now, for you shall hunger.' (chapter 6, verses 24f). No other evangelist tells us that Jesus said these things.

This does not mean that Luke was inventing these stories out of his own dislike of rich people. Mark too made clear Jesus's view of and fears for the rich. Luke took from him one of Jesus's most frightening sayings. After Jesus had told the rich man to sell all his goods and give them to the poor (see above), the man's face fell. He became sad, says Luke, 'for he was very rich'. Jesus then said, 'How hard it is for those who have riches to enter into the kingdom of God! It is easier for a camel to go through the eye of a needle than for a rich man to enter the kingdom of God.'

Christina Onassis, daughter of the shipping magnate Aristotle Onassis.

Jesus did not say that this was impossible and that all rich people were doomed. Hearing him, his followers asked him, 'Then who can be saved?' Jesus answered, 'What is impossible with men is possible with God.' (chapter 18, verses 24 to 27)

Like Mark, Luke also records an incident in the Jerusalem Temple. Jesus saw the rich putting their gifts into the Temple treasury. Then he saw a poor widow put in two copper coins. And he said, 'Truly I tell you, this poor widow has put in more than all of them; for they all contributed out of their abundance, but she out of her poverty put in all the living she had.' (chapter 21, verses 1 to 4)

Jesus knew that the rich, pouring out comparatively huge sums of money in good causes, often sacrifice very little. The poor sometimes give their all.

The absurd desire for possessions

Although this part of Jesus's teaching is found in the other gospels, nobody emphasises it so much as Luke. Here are two of Jesus's stories, recorded by Luke alone, about foolish rich men.

> The land of a rich man brought forth plentifully; and he thought to himself, 'What shall I do, for I have nowhere to store my crops?' And he said, 'I will do this: I will pull down my barns, and build larger ones; and there I will store all my grain and my goods. And I will say to my soul, "Soul, you have ample goods laid up for many years; take your ease, eat, drink and be merry."' But God said to him, 'Fool! This night your soul is required of you; and the things you have prepared, whose will they be?'
>
> Jesus's comment was, 'So is he who lays up treasure for himself, and is not rich towards God.'
>
> (chapter 12, verses 16 to 21)

Today people will still go to absurd lengths simply for possessions. The *Independent* newspaper recently had the following article on the sale of the Picasso painting shown opposite.

Record £13.7m is paid for 'Blue' Picasso

A BLUE PERIOD Picasso painting entitled *Maternité*, a modern update of the traditional image of *Virgin and Child*, became the most expensive twentieth century work of art sold at auction when it made $24.75m (£13.7m) at Christie's in New York on Monday night.

Picasso's blue-draped mother, painted without distortion, is the product of his studies in the Louvre, her sewing which lies beside her gives her a modern aspect while the standing child clutches the ball he has been playing with. It dates from 1901. Blue Period works have almost disappeared from the market – it is a great rarity.

Independent, 15 November 1988

Can any painting, however rare, be worth 'fighting over'?

When one man and his brother were arguing about dividing up goods they had been left, Jesus refused to help them, even though they begged him to. Instead he warned them, 'Take heed, and beware of covetousness; for a man's life does not consist of the abundance of his possessions.' (chapter 12, verses 13 to 15)

Dives and Lazarus

The second story is about a rich man, often called Dives, and a beggar named Lazarus. The rich man eats fabulously every day. Lazarus would love the crumbs that fall from his table, but all he gets is dogs licking his sores.

Then both die. In heaven Lazarus is comforted by the father of the Jews, Abraham. The rich man is in torment. He begs Abraham to send

Lazarus to dip the end of his finger in water and to cool his tongue with it. Abraham's answer is that the rich man has already tasted his pleasures on earth. There is no way now in which the two can meet.

At last the rich man shows some care for others. He begs Abraham to let his five brothers who are still on earth know of the torment that awaits them if they do not mend their ways. Abraham refuses, pointing out that the great figures of the Jewish past — Moses and the prophets — have already insisted that the poor must be cared for. 'If they do not hear Moses and the prophets,' he says, 'neither will they be convinced if some one should rise from the dead.'

Read this story (chapter 16, verses 19 to 31) in the light of the following two comments made by Professor William Barclay:

> 'The sin of Dives was that he could look on the world's suffering and need and feel no answering sword of grief and pity pierce his heart; he looked at his fellow-man, hungry and in pain, and did nothing about it. His was the punishment of the man who never noticed.
>
> It seems hard that his request that his brothers should be warned was refused. But it is the plain fact that if men possess the truth of God's word, and if, wherever they look, there is sorrow to be comforted, need to be supplied, pain to be relieved, and it moves them to no feeling and no action, nothing will change them.'
>
> (William Barclay, *The Gospel of Luke*, Saint Andrew Press, Edinburgh 1975, p. 214)

The power of prayer

Luke is also fascinated by the power of prayer. His gospel shows Jesus not only praying himself but also teaching his disciples how to pray.

Praying for the help of God, he believed, made people stronger. He warned his followers that they would often be tempted to give in to weakness and the cares of the world. 'Watch at all times,' he told them, 'praying that you may have strength to escape all these things that will take place.' (chapter 21, verse 36)

One of his parables urged his followers to persist in their prayers and not to give up in despair.

> In a certain city there was a judge who neither feared God nor regarded man; and there was a widow in that city who kept coming to him and saying, 'Vindicate me against my adversary.' For a while he refused; but afterward he said to himself, 'Though I neither fear God nor regard man, yet because this widow bothers me, I will vindicate her, or she will wear me out by her continual coming.'

Jesus commented, 'Will not God vindicate his elect, who cry to him

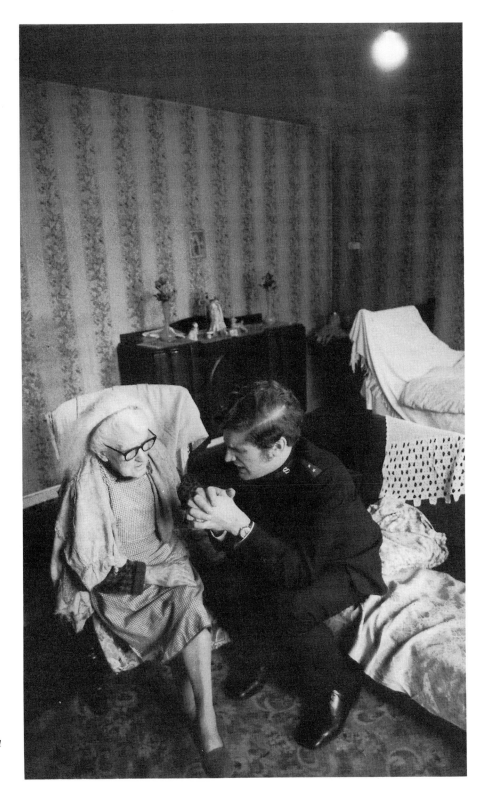

An officer of the Salvation Army prays with an old lady. What do you think they are praying for?

day and night?' By 'his elect' he meant those God had chosen as his people. They might live in an evil world, but in the end God's will must triumph. As Luke observed, this parable taught 'that they ought always to pray and not lose heart'. (chapter 18, verses 1 to 8)

Jesus teaches his followers to pray

Luke tells us that Jesus himself prayed before he was baptised; that he would go by himself into the mountains to pray; that sometimes his followers would interrupt him when he wanted to pray alone.

He once took his three closest disciples — Peter, James and John — onto a mountain with him whilst he prayed.

And not surprisingly, on one occasion when he had just finished praying, his disciples said to him, 'Lord, teach us to pray, as John taught his disciples.'

The prayer Jesus taught them has become so famous in the Church that it is today known as the Lord's prayer. Christians use it when they pray privately and when they pray together in acts of worship.

Luke tells us that Jesus taught his followers to say:

> Father,
> hallowed be thy name.
> Thy kingdom come.
> Give us each day our daily bread;
> and forgive us our sins,
> for we ourselves forgive every one who is indebted to us;
> and lead us not into temptation.
>
> (chapter 11, verses 1 to 4)

The Lord's prayer

Matthew's gospel also records this prayer, in a slightly different and longer form (Matthew chapter 6, verses 9 to 13). Many scholars think that Matthew's version is a later one, written down when Christians had added to and developed Jesus's original prayer.

Let's look at each line of this prayer as we read it in Luke's gospel:

Father

Jesus himself called God his father. Hardly anyone else in his nation had ever done so. The Bible which he knew refers to God as a father only fourteen times. Addressing God by this name expresses the belief that God loves the Jewish people like a father loves his child, tenderly, even when they have disobeyed God's laws.

'My dear son ... my darling child', one passage in the Old Testament reads:

'... as often as I speak against him,
I do remember him still.
Therefore my heart yearns for him;
I will surely have mercy on him,' says the Lord.

(Jeremiah chapter 31 verse 20)

This is the view of God's love which Jesus believed in. Now he is encouraging his followers to see God in the same way.

Another thought which Jesus put to his followers makes this even clearer. Imagine a friend arriving at your house at midnight, desperate for something to eat. You have nothing in the house and therefore rush round to another friend to borrow three loaves — but your other friend is already in bed, along with his children. At first no one will come to the door, however hard you knock. But if you keep on knocking, sooner or later your friend will be forced to get out of bed and give you the loaves.

Is God like this when we pray to him? Not really. At the end of this story Jesus added, 'What father among you, if his son asks for a fish, will instead of a fish give him a serpent; or if he asks for an egg, will give him a scorpion? If you then, who are evil, know how to give good gifts to your children, how much more will the heavenly Father give the Holy Spirit to those who ask him?' God is much more like a loving father than a friend who would rather stay in bed than help us out of our difficulties.

According to Luke, Jesus wants to emphasis two things here:

God's generous love;
our need not to give up too easily when we pray to him.

'Ask and it will be given you,' says Jesus; 'seek, and you will find; knock, and it will be opened to you. For every one who asks receives, and he who seeks finds, and to him who knocks it will be opened.' (chapter 11, verses 5 to 13)

Let God's name be holy

The next request — 'Hallowed be your name', which means 'Let your name be specially sacred' — seems at first odd. Surely God's name is special and sacred.

But do people really care about it? Is God supremely important to them? What those who say this prayer are asking for is some action from God which will make the whole world recognise his greatness.

So the prayer leads us immediately onto the next request: that God's rule will come on earth.

And let his kingdom come

In making such a prayer to God we are also offering our own lives to help the kingdom of God to come on earth. All those parts of our own lives which are opposed to the kingdom of God are to be crushed. And we must give all our strength to working on behalf of all that God's kingdom stands for: the triumph of good over evil, of love over hatred, of care for others over care for our own selves.

Our daily bread

This makes the next request a strange one. It seems to be entirely selfish. Are we here simply asking God to look after us.

Look more carefully. Some words of Bishop John Moorman make it clear that selfishness is far from Jesus's prayer here. 'Though we pray for physical benefits, we pray only for the simplest thing — bread, the staple diet of the western world,' he wrote. 'Moreover, we ask for only a very limited supply, enough to support life for a single day.' (John R H Moorman, *The Path to Glory*, SPCK 1963, p. 132)

Who in your view is responsible for the plight of these young people? Can you suggest ways of helping them?

So again, as we make this request of God our father, we make a moral demand on our own selves. God feeds us, and at the same time insists that we take only what we need.

Most of us in the western world have far more than this. At the same time, countless millions of our human brothers and sisters are starving. A headline in the *Independent* on 11 November 1988 read: 'Sudanese Face Starvation or War'. The article continued:

> Half the people fleeing from civil war in southern Sudan in the past seven months may have died before they reached safety, Christopher Patten, Minister for Overseas Development, said yesterday after visiting refugee camps in western Ethiopia.
>
> It was one of the worst human tragedies of the past few decades, he said. 'A typical story would be a family group who had travelled up to four months, tacking back and forth across Sudan trying to avoid armed Muslim tribes, the Sudan army or marauding gangs, and living off leaves, berries, nuts or roots they had grubbed up.'

Is it right to ask God to give us enough bread for each day, without making sure that such people as the Sudanese will have more to live on than 'leaves, berries, nuts or roots they had grubbed up'?

Forgiveness

The plea for forgiveness in the Lord's Prayer also contains a condition. We ask to be forgiven in exactly the same way as we forgive others. 'Forgive us our sins, for we ourselves forgive every one who is indebted to us.'

Elsewhere in his gospel Luke quotes some powerful words of Jesus on this subject:

> Judge not, and you will not be judged; condemn not, and you will not be condemned; forgive, and you will be forgiven; give, and it will be given to you; good measure, pressed down, shaken together, running over, will be put into your lap. For the measure you give will be the measure you get back.
>
> (chapter 6, verses 37f)

Temptation

The last request in this prayer is one of the oddest: 'lead us not into temptation'. Jesus himself, as we shall see (pages 102–103), was tempted. The problem about temptation to do evil is not that it occurs, but that it's difficult for us to resist it. Does it matter that some evil thing attracts us, so long as we turn aside from it?

Jesus and outcasts

Without Luke we would not know that Jesus once stood up on behalf of an outcast woman in the house of a self-righteous man who despised her. She kissed Jesus's feet and poured precious ointment on them. Jesus read the man's thoughts and said to him, 'Her sins, which are many, are forgiven, for she loved much.' He also added what was clearly a criticism of the unforgiving man himself: 'but he who is forgiven little, loves little'. (chapter 7, verses 36 to 50)

Many were shocked by Jesus's friendship with such sinful people. Jesus defended himself by telling a famous story which we find nowhere else but in Luke:

> There was a man who had two sons; and the younger of them said to his father, 'Father, give me the share of the property that falls to me.' And he divided his living between them. Not many days later, the younger son gathered all he had and took his journey into a far country, and there he squandered all his property in loose living.

Soon, in Jesus's story, the young man falls on extremely hard times. All his money spent, he finds a job feeding pigs, wishing he could eat the pig swill himself. Finally he decides to go back to his father and ask for a job.

The story continues:

> . . . he arose and came to his father. But while he was yet at a distance, his father saw him and had compassion, and ran and embraced him and kissed him.

The young man's father dresses his second son in beautiful clothes, puts rings on his fingers and arranges a great feast. The elder brother is annoyed, refusing to come to the feast, complaining to his father that while he has been a loyal servant, his brother wasted everything. His father replies:

> Son, you are always with me, and all that is mine is yours. It was fitting to make merry and be glad, for this your brother was dead, and is alive; he was lost and is found.
>
> (chapter 15, verses 11 to 32)

To drive home the point that even those who have been 'lost' are welcome in the eyes of Jesus — and God — just before telling this story he told another one:

> . . . what woman, having ten silver coins, if she loses one coin, does not light a lamp and sweep the house and seek diligently until she finds it? And when she has found it, she calls together her friends

and neighbours, saying, 'Rejoice with me, for I have found the coin which I had lost.'

(chapter 15, verses 8 to 10)

These two stories (or 'parables' as they are called — see page 81), are found only in Luke's gospel.

Jesus and women

In a way not found in any other gospel, Luke loved to portray Jesus's tenderness towards women (as we have already partly seen, on pages 9–10). We learn from Luke that women would receive him and his disciples into their homes and look after them. Jesus would take the chance to teach them. In response, Luke shows, they stayed with him to the very end, even though his male disciples had run away when their master was on trial and about to be crucified.

Martha and Mary

Amongst Jesus's friends were two sisters named Martha and Mary. Luke tells us that Martha welcomed Jesus and his followers into her house:

> And she had a sister named Mary, who sat at the Lord's feet and listened to his teaching. But Martha was distracted with much serving; and she went to him and said, 'Lord, do you not care that my sister has left me to serve alone? Tell her then to help me.'

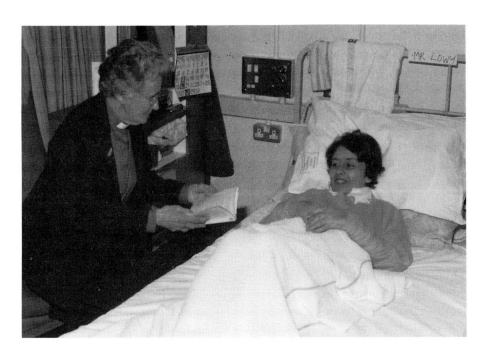

Here is one woman, representing the Church, giving strength to another.

But the Lord answered her, 'Martha, Martha, you are anxious and troubled about many things; one thing is needful. Mary has chosen the good portion, which shall not be taken away from her.'

(chapter 10, verses 38 to 42)

The forgiven prostitute

The concern of Jesus for women is not something unique to Luke's gospel. One story Luke tells to demonstrate this concern is about a prostitute. It occurs in different forms in all three other gospels.

Yet if you compare these four versions, you discover that Luke presents a far more loving, forgiving and caring Jesus than the other three. More: because it was so important for him, he transferred it from its place in the other gospels to a position close to the beginning of Jesus's ministry.

This is Luke's version of the episode:

> One of the Pharisees [see pages 66–67 on these] asked him to eat with him, and he went into the Pharisee's house, and took his place at table. And behold, a woman of the city, who was a sinner, when she learned that he was at table in the Pharisee's house, brought an alabaster flask of ointment, and standing behind him at his feet, weeping, she began to wet his feet with her tears, and wiped them with the hair of her head, and kissed his feet, and anointed them with the ointment. Now when the Pharisee who had invited him saw it, he said to himself, 'If this man were a prophet, he would have known who and what sort of woman this is who is touching him, for she is a sinner.' And Jesus answering him said to him, 'Simon, I have something to say to you.' And he answered, 'What is it, Teacher?' 'A certain creditor had two debtors; one owed five hundred denarii, and the other fifty. When they could not pay, he forgave them both. Now which of them will love him more?' Simon answered, 'The one, I suppose, to whom he forgave more.' And he said to him, 'You have judged rightly.' Then turning toward the woman he said to Simon, 'Do you see this woman? I entered your house, you gave me no water for my feet, but she has wet my feet with her tears and wiped them with her hair. You gave me no kiss, but from the time I came in she has not ceased to kiss my feet. You did not anoint my head with oil, but she has anointed my feet with ointment. Therefore I tell you, her sins, which are many, are forgiven, for she loved much; but he who is forgiven little, loves little.' And he said to her, 'Your sins are forgiven.' Then those who were at table with him began to say among themselves, 'Who is this, who even forgives sins?' And he said to the woman, 'Your faith has saved you; go in peace.'

(chapter 7, verses 36 to 50)

Now read the other three versions:

54

Mark's version chapter 14, verses 3 to 9

And while he was at Bethany in the house of Simon the leper, as he sat at table, a woman came with an alabaster flask of ointment of pure nard, very costly, and she broke the flask and poured it over his head. But there were some who said to themselves indignantly, 'Why was the ointment thus wasted? For this ointment might have been sold for more than three hundred denarii, and given to the poor.' And they reproached her. But Jesus said, 'Let her alone; why do you trouble her? She has done a beautiful thing to me. For you always have the poor with you, and whenever you will, you can do good to them; but you will not always have me. She has done what she could; she has anointed my body beforehand for burying. And truly, I say to you, wherever the gospel is preached in the whole world, what she has done will be told in memory of her.'

Matthew's version chapter 26, verses 6 to 13

Now when Jesus was at Bethany in the house of Simon the leper, a woman came up to him with an alabaster flask of very expensive ointment, and she poured it on his head as he sat at table. But when the disciples saw it, they were indignant, saying, 'Why this waste? For this ointment might have been sold for a large sum, and given to the poor.' But Jesus, aware of this, said to them, 'Why do you trouble the woman? For she has done a beautiful thing to me. For you always have the poor with you, but you will not always have me. In pouring this ointment on my body she has done it to prepare me for burial. Truly, I say to you, wherever the gospel is preached in the whole world, what she has done will be told in memory of her.'

John's version chapter 12, verses 1 to 8

Six days before the Passover, Jesus came to Bethany, where Lazarus was, whom Jesus had raised from the dead. There they made him a supper; Martha served, and Lazarus was one of those at table with him. Mary took a pound of costly ointment of pure nard and anointed the feet of Jesus and wiped his feet with her hair; and the house was filled with the fragrance of the ointment. But Judas Iscariot, one of his disciples (he who was to betray him), said, 'Why was this ointment not sold for three hundred denarii and given to the poor?' This he said, not that he cared for the poor but because he was a thief, and as he had the money box he used to take what was put into it. Jesus said, 'Let her alone, let her keep it for the day of my burial. The poor you always have with you, but you do not always have me.'

These are all recognisably the same story, but the different ways in which each gospel-writer uses it are astonishing.

In addition, Luke puts in the middle of his story another one — about a man who forgives his debtors — for the woman Jesus shows compassion to is 'a sinner'.

Finally, what is absolutely clear is that Luke also shows Jesus displaying a remarkable tenderness towards the sinful woman, a tenderness nowhere brought out by the other three gospels.

Women played a very important part in the life of Jesus. Look at the role of women in the world today. How does it differ from their role at the time of Jesus?

Assignments

K U 1 Luke paints his own portrait of Jesus. By reference to his gospel, write a description of Luke's Jesus. Compare your character study with that of your neighbour. Do they differ in any way?

E 2 When Mary knew that she was to give birth she sang:
> He has put down the mighty from their thrones,
> and exalted those of low degree;
> he has filled the hungry with good things.

Express these thoughts in your own words. Do you think they have a message for us today?

K 3 What does Luke teach us about Jesus's attitude to the rich? Relate two stories found only in Luke's gospel which tell us about foolish rich men.

E 4 What are your views about wealth? Do you think that any one person should be able to afford £13.7 million for a painting?

E 5 'A man's life does not consist of the abundance of his possessions.' How far do you agree with this statement?

U 6 Read the Lord's Prayer in Luke chapter 11, verses 1 to 4. What do we learn about Jesus's teaching from this prayer?

E 7 'Give us each day our daily bread.' Do you think this is a selfish request? Think especially about the hungry in the world.

K U 8 Read the article on page 51 (*Independent*, 11 November 1988). If we wish to be assured that God will give us enough bread for each day, what must we do to make sure that such people as the Sudanese will have more to live on than "leaves, berries, nuts or roots"?

K 9 In groups gather together all the information you can about those people who are hungry and homeless in the world. Refer to newspapers and perhaps religious journals. Visit your local library.

K U 10 What does Luke tell us about forgiveness? Explain the words, 'but he who is forgiven little, loves little.'

KU 11 Write a modern version of the parable of the Prodigal Son (Luke chapter 15, verses 11 to 32). The scribes and the Pharisees had been complaining about Jesus's 'lax' attitude towards sinners. How does this parable answer their complaint? This parable links up with another which is found only in Luke's gospel. What is it?

U 12 Read Luke chapter 7, verses 36 to 50. Why, in your opinion, was the woman forgiven?

U 13 Read the three other versions of Luke chapter 7, verses 36 to 50, as found in Mark's gospel (chapter 14, verses 3 to 9), Matthew's gospel (chapter 26, verses 6 to 13) and John's gospel (chapter 12, verses 1 to 8). How do they differ?

KUE 14 Some jobs in our society are reserved solely for men.
(a) List some of these.
(b) Do you think women could do them just as well as men?
(c) What are the different strengths of women and men?
(d) Should those churches which do not allow women to become priests change their minds?

◀ *Deacon Sylvia Match was the first woman to conduct a Church of England ceremony in Britain.*

Visiting American priest The Rev Suzanne ▶
Fageol celebrates the Eucharist in London.

4 Friends and enemies of Jesus

John the Baptist

Luke reveals that some people thought John the Baptist was the Christ. John denied it. His description of the coming of the Christ, bringing judgement to the world as well as salvation, was extremely vivid. 'I baptize you with water,' he said; 'but he who is mightier than I is coming, the thongs of whose sandals I am not worthy to untie; he will baptize you with the Holy Spirit and with fire. His winnowing fork is in his hand, to clear his threshing floor and to gather the wheat into his granary, but the chaff he will burn with unquenchable fire.' (chapter 3, verses 15 to 17)

Wheat consists of the ears of corn which can be ground up and made into bread or eaten in some other way; the chaff is that part of the plant which surrounds the ears but cannot be eaten. According to John the Baptist, therefore, the coming of Jesus will divide people into two sorts: his valuable friends who accept his message and teaching; and his worthless enemies who reject him. The first are wheat; the second group are chaff.

Levi the tax collector

We have already seen how Luke shows that Jesus was specially concerned to save outcasts. The first person he called to follow him is a startling example of this, for he was a tax collector, Levi.

The tax collectors were looked upon as the lowest of the low in Jewish society. In the first place they collected taxes for the hated Romans, who ruled over the Jews. In the second place they always collected more taxes than they were entitled to, so as to enrich themselves. In the third place they often did so by force. So much were tax collectors hated by their fellow-Jews that they were not even allowed into the synagogues to worship God.

This is how Jesus called Levi to follow him:

He went out, and saw a tax collector, named Levi, sitting at the tax

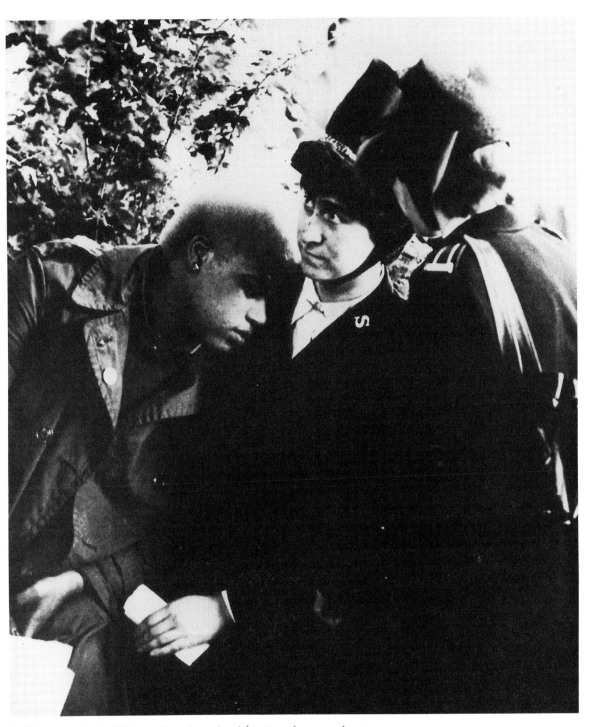

A Salvation Army Officer offers her shoulder to a down-and-out.

office; and he said to him, 'Follow me.' And he left everything, and rose and followed him.

Many criticised Jesus for associating with such a man. In a powerful statement found only in Luke's gospel, Jesus argued: 'Those who are well have no need of a physician, but only those who are sick.' He added: 'I have not come to call the righteous, but sinners to repentance.' (chapter 5, verses 27f and 30f)

Leaving everything behind

Levi 'left everything', and instantly followed Jesus. In Luke's gospel we see Jesus demanding instant obedience. To another man he said, 'Follow me.' Unlike Levi, the man replied, 'Lord, let me first go and bury my father.' The stern response of Jesus was, 'Leave the dead to bury their own dead but as for you, go and proclaim the kingdom of God.' (chapter 9, verses 59f)

Apostles and disciples

Many others were attracted to Jesus. Luke calls them 'disciples' which means pupils. From these, after a night of prayer, he chose twelve.

Why twelve? As we saw earlier, for many centuries the Jewish people — God's special people — had been divided into twelve tribes. Jesus was choosing an inner group who would establish the new people of God, to include not just the Jews but any who accepted him and his teaching.

An 'apostle' means someone sent on a special mission. Men sent to represent their own land in another country were called 'apostles'. So were those entrusted with important messages. It isn't difficult to see why Jesus chose this term for his twelve closest disciples.

Later in Luke's gospel we read that Jesus gave them remarkable powers. Like Jesus they were enabled to cure diseases. He gave them 'authority over all demons'. Luke says, 'He sent them out to preach the kingdom of God and to heal.'

Just as the coming of Jesus divided people into those willing to accept him (the wheat) and those who turned against him (the chaff), so the mission of the twelve apostles separated the good from the bad. Jesus told them to enter any house willing to receive them. He added, 'And wherever they do not receive you, when you leave that town, shake off the dust from your feet as a testimony against them.' (chapter 9, verses 1 to 6)

Jesus's real family

These twelve apostles, and men and women like them, now became Jesus's family. Even his family by blood had to understand this; Luke writes that once:

> . . . his mother and his brothers came to him, but they could not reach him for the crowd. And he was told, 'Your mother and your brothers are standing outside, desiring to see you.' But he said to them, 'My mother and my brothers are those who hear the word of God and do it.'
>
> (chapter 8, verses 19 to 21)

To belong to the family of Jesus demands utter obedience to God's will. Another time, Luke says, a woman in a crowd around Jesus shouted, 'Blessed is the womb that bore you, and the breasts that you sucked!' Jesus made almost exactly the same reply as before: 'Blessed rather are those who hear the word of God and keep it!' (chapter 11, verses 27f)

These are strange words, for we normally cling to our families and respect and care for our parents. When a huge mass of people were following him, Jesus turned to them and said, 'If anyone comes to me and does not hate his father and mother and wife and children and brothers and sisters, yes, and even his own life, he cannot be my disciple.' Jesus is not ordering us to be cruel to all our earthly relatives. What he means is revealed a few verses later. We should, he says, be attached to nothing and no one more than to God and his laws. 'So therefore, whoever of you does not renounce all that he has cannot be my disciple.' (chapter 14, verses 26 and 33)

The cost of following Jesus

Jesus explained to his apostles that following him also meant suffering as he did. 'If any man would come after me, let him deny himself and take up his cross daily and follow me,' he told them.

The idea of 'taking up a cross' obviously comes from Jesus's own coming crucifixion. Later in the gospel we read that when Jesus was ordered to carry his huge wooden cross to the place where he was executed, the guards 'seized one Simon of Cyrene, who was coming in from the country, and laid on him the cross, to carry it behind Jesus' (chapter 23, verse 26). Simon of Cyrene is obviously a pattern for all those who want to become Christians and follow Jesus.

But taking up your cross 'daily' extends the idea of being crucified into our everyday lives. It is a permanent pattern of life. Instead of letting our own desires always have their way, we are to crucify them.

Jesus insisted that this was the only way to achieve true happiness. Looking after ourselves and indulging our own desires is not the right way. 'Whoever would save his life will lose it,' he declared; 'and whoever loses his life for my sake, he will save it.' He added a question: 'What does it profit a man if he gains the whole world and loses or forfeits himself?' (chapter 9, verses 23 to 27)

A new way of life

Following Jesus thus involved a completely new way of life. First it involved giving up earthly possessions. 'Sell your possessions, and give alms,' he told them; 'provide yourselves with purses that do not grow old, with a treasure in the heavens that does not fail, where no thief approaches and no moth destroys.' He added, 'For where your treasure is, there will your heart be also.' (chapter 12, verses 33f)

Secondly, Jesus taught, all of his followers needed to turn aside from their sins (to 'repent') or else they would perish. Eighteen people had recently been killed when a tower at a place called Siloam fell down. There were some who believed that these eighteen people must have been especially wicked to perish in this way. Jesus disagreed. 'Do you think that they were worse offenders than all the others who dwelt in Jerusalem?' he asked. 'I tell you, No; but unless you repent you will all likewise perish.' (chapter 13, verses 4f)

We see both these commands put into practice when Jesus was welcomed by the principal tax collector Zacchaeus. 'Behold, Lord, the half of my goods I give to the poor,' said Zacchaeus; 'and if I have defrauded anyone of anything, I restore it fourfold.' Jesus said to him, 'Today salvation is come to this house.' (chapter 19, verses 1 to 10)

Zacchaeus repents of his previous greed and ill doing; and he makes up for it by giving away his ill-gotten gains.

Disciples will be rejected, as Jesus was

Though Jesus was often rejected, he refused to seek any sort of revenge. Once, on his way to Jerusalem, he sent messengers to a village in Samaria, hoping to find lodgings, but the people would not receive him. (This was because he was going to the Jewish capital city, Jerusalem, and the Jews and Samaritans at that time hated each other.) When his disciples James and John saw this, they wanted to pray that fire would descend from heaven and burn up the village. But Jesus rebuked them, and they went to another village.

This same kind of rejection was soon experienced by the seventy disciples Jesus sent out to preach about him. Jesus told them that being rejected like this meant that they were extremely close to him. 'He who hears you hears me, and he who rejects you rejects me,' he said. (chapter 9, verses 51 to 55, and chapter 10, verses 1 to 16)

Homeless too

To be homeless, Luke tells us, was also a likely fate for anyone who followed Jesus. From the age of thirty, when Jesus began his ministry, he had no permanent home. Luke describes how he was approached by a man who said, 'I will follow you wherever you go.' Jesus's response was, 'Foxes have holes, and birds of the air have nests; but the Son of man has nowhere to lay his head.' (chapter 9, verses 57f)

Even put to death

The persecution which Jesus suffered, he said, is a pattern for the persecution his disciples will also suffer. Their closest blood relatives will betray them. 'You will be delivered up even by parents and brothers and kinsmen and friends, and some of you they will put to death,' he forecast; 'you will be hated by all for my name's sake.' (chapter 21, verses 16f)

Those who reject Jesus

For many, Jesus's demands were too much. Others began to hate him. They included the following groups of religious people who ought to have welcomed him.

The scribes

The scribes are constantly portrayed in Luke's gospel as the enemies of Jesus. This group of men spent much time studying the Jewish scriptures. They were experts in legal matters, as well as being always ready to explain any difficult question about the Bible.

Since all they taught was drawn from the books of the Bible, they were deeply disturbed when Jesus came claiming to speak with as much authority as their beloved scriptures.

One day, Luke tells us, as Jesus was teaching in the Jerusalem Temple, 'the chief priests and the scribes with the elders came up and said to him, "Tell us by what authority you do these things or who it is that gave you this authority?' The scribes had refused to accept the teaching of John the Baptist yet he had been extremely popular. So instead of answering the scribes' question, Jesus simply asked them who gave John his authority, and the scribes backed away and would not answer his question. (chapter 20, verses 1ff)

Jesus accused them of being hypocrites — that is, people who pretend to be decent and good but really conceal their true aims. Deep down, he said, the scribes wanted not to live righteous and decent lives in the sight of God, but to receive human praise. 'Beware of the scribes, who like to go about in long robes, and love salutations in the market places and the best seats in the synagogues and the places of honour at feasts, who devour widow's houses and for a pretence make long prayers. They will receive the greater condemnation.' (chapter 20, verses 45 to 47)

In Luke's gospel we find Jesus consistently attacking such arrogance and vanity. 'When you are invited by anyone to a marriage feast,' he advised, 'do not sit down in a place of honour, lest a more eminent man than you be invited by him; and he who invited you both will come and say to you, "Give place to this man," and then you will begin with shame to take the lowest place.' Jesus said we should first take the lowest place, and our host will then invite us to go up higher.

He said this not simply as a piece of worldly advice but to show the proper attitude of humility which everyone ought to display before their fellow men and women, and before God. (chapter 14, verses 7 to 11)

The Pharisees

Luke often depicts the scribes ganging up against Jesus in the company of another deeply religious group of that time — the Pharisees. Like the scribes, the Pharisees scoured the scriptures for rules for their everyday life. Jesus accused them of following trivial rules but neglecting justice and the love of God. Just as he accused the scribes of being hypocrites, so he said that the Pharisees loved 'the best seats in the synagogues and salutations in the market place'. (chapter 11, verses 42f)

As we have seen, the Pharisees condemned Jesus for befriending such people as the sinner who anointed him with costly ointment and wet his feet with her tears. They despised tax collectors like Levi. Jesus therefore told a story about a Pharisee and a tax collector who both went to pray in the Temple. The Pharisee's prayer was really a stream of self-congratulation. He said, 'God, I thank thee that I am not like other men, extortioners, unjust, adulterers, or even like this tax collector. I fast twice a week, I give tithes of all I get.' But the tax collector would not even lift up his eyes to heaven. Instead he beat his breast and said, 'God, be merciful to me, a sinner.' Jesus commented that it was the tax collector, not the Pharisee, who went home forgiven by God. 'Everyone who exalts himself will be humbled,' he declared, 'but he who humbles himself will be exalted.' (chapter 18, verses 9 to 14)

The Pharisees and the sabbath

So keen were the Pharisees to observe every law to the letter that they would not lift a finger on the sabbath day. This was the seventh day of the week when, according to the law of Moses no one was to work. The Pharisees held that this meant that they could not even do a good deed on the sabbath. Jesus disagreed. He was dining with a Pharisee one sabbath when a man suffering dropsy was brought to him. Jesus asked, 'Is it lawful to heal on the sabbath day or not?' No one answered. So Jesus healed the man. He then asked, 'Which of you, having a son or an ox that has fallen into a well, will not immediately pull him out on a sabbath day?' Luke records that 'they could not reply to this'. (chapter 14, verses 1 to 6)

Yet in spite of these criticisms and disagreements, it is interesting that in Luke's gospel we find Jesus dining with Pharisees. No other gospel writer tells us that some Pharisees came to warn Jesus to leave the neighbourhood of Jerusalem because a Roman ruler, Herod, was planning to kill him. (chapter 13, verse 31)

Whereas Matthew's gospel displays a powerfully felt bitterness about many of Jesus's fellow-Jews, Luke has none of this. Even the scribes, he reveals, sometimes appreciated and agreed with what Jesus said. 'Teacher,' they once said to him, 'you have spoken well.'

This was after Jesus had disagreed with a group known as the Sadducees about whether or not men and women can receive new life after death.

The Sadducees

These Sadducees were Jews who accepted as God's teaching only the first five books of our Bible. In these books there appears no belief in a future life, so the Sadducees refused to believe in it either.

Jesus, along with the Pharisees and other Jews of his time, did believe in life after death. So, some Sadducees asked him what would happen if one woman married in all seven brothers, one after the other as each one died. 'In the resurrection, therefore, whose wife will the woman be,' they wanted to know, 'for the seven had her as wife?'

Obviously they wished to make Jesus's belief in a future life seem foolish. Jesus however replied that there is no such thing as marriage in heaven. And he said that they ought to remember that God had declared himself to be the God of three great Jewish forefathers — Abraham, Isaac and Jacob — long after those three men were dead. 'Now he is not God of the dead, but of the living,' Jesus argued, 'for all live in him.' This was the answer which pleased the scribes. (chapter 20, verses 27 to 40)

The religious leaders of the Jews

These men included those who ministered in the Jerusalem Temple and were known as high priests or simply priests, as well as a group of seventy elders who with the high priest of the time formed the Jerusalem Council. It was this Council which decided that Jesus was mocking God by implying that he was the Christ, the Son of God. (chapter 22, verses 66 to 71)

Even when such men were plotting to kill him, Jesus's compassion did not desert him. Luke tells us that when the high priest's followers came to seize him, one of his disciples drew a sword and struck the high priest's servant, cutting off his ear. Jesus said, 'No more of this!', touched the servant's ear and healed him. (chapter 22, verses 49 to 51)

The high priest alone had the right to enter the holiest part of the Jerusalem Temple once a year. Some seven thousand country priests served in the Temple by rotation. The other assistants of the high priest were called Levites; their tasks included bringing wood and water to the Temple and providing its music.

Although many of these men turned against Jesus, again Luke refuses to condemn all priests and religious leaders. In fact his gospel begins with the announcement by the angel Gabriel to a priest named Zechariah that his wife Elizabeth would give birth to a child, John the Baptist, even though Elizabeth was well past the age for conceiving children. Luke describes Zechariah and his wife as 'both righteous before God, walking in all the commandments of the Lord blameless'. (chapter 1, verse 6)

The Samaritans

Jews and Samaritans at this time were in conflict. They had built rival temples — the Jews in Jerusalem, the Samaritans on Mount Gerizim. The Samaritans took particular pleasure in blocking the path of Jews who wanted to travel from Galilee across their country (Samaria) to Jerusalem to attend religious festivals there. Jesus was shunned by a Samaritan village on just such a journey. (chapter 9, verses 51 to 53)

It is therefore typical of Luke that he makes a Samaritan a hero of one of his stories. On the way to Jerusalem, he tells us, Jesus was passing along between Samaria and Galilee. As he entered a village ten lepers met him, begging him to have mercy on them. He told them to go and show themselves to the priest — who had the authority to declare a former leper clean again. On the way they were all cleansed.

'Then one of them,' the story continues, 'when he saw that he was healed, turned back, praising God with a loud voice; and he fell on his face at Jesus's feet, giving him thanks.' Luke adds: 'Now he was a Samaritan.'

> Then said Jesus, 'Were not ten cleansed? Where are the nine. Was no one found to return and give praise to God except this foreigner?' And he said to him, 'Rise and go your way; your faith has made you well.'
>
> (chapter 17, verses 11 to 19)

Samaritans, though 'foreigners' and disliked by many Jews, are here revealed as sometimes more capable of responding to him than his own people. Here is also therefore another hint of how the gospel as seen by Luke is to reach all nations.

The Romans

Herod Antipas

A Herod was ruling Judea, Luke tells us, when Jesus was born. His son, Herod Antipas, was to play a part in bringing Jesus to the cross.

Luke represents him as a fundamentally evil man. Jesus calls him a fox. He had married his own brother's wife, and when John the Baptist condemned him for this and other wicked ways, Herod first of all imprisoned John and then beheaded him.

Herod Antipas had a hand in Jesus's trial, according to Luke. Yet because Luke wishes to show that the Roman government has nothing to fear from Jesus's followers, he tells us that Herod did not find him guilty. Even so, Herod allowed his soldiers to mock Jesus and he himself treated Jesus with contempt. (chapter 23, verses 6 to 16)

Pontius Pilate

The Roman governor (or 'procurator') of Judea between AD 26 and 36 was named Pontius Pilate. Pilate had very much offended the Jews by allowing Roman soldiers to march in battle order into Jerusalem, carrying their military standards. Although he found Jesus innocent, declaring, 'I find no crime in this man,' nevertheless he was weak enough to hand him over to his enemies, to be crucified. (chapter 23, verses 1 to 5 and 13 to 25)

Where did it all take place?

In the synagogues

There were synagogues in every Jewish town, places for worshipping God and studying his words as they were found in the Bible and in Jewish traditions.

Elders ran them, and these appointed a 'ruler of the synagogue' to take charge of the worship. He could invite any man to speak, if he thought him learned enough.

The main act of worship at the synagogue occurred on the sabbath day (Saturday). Prayers and readings from both the laws and the writings of the prophets always took place at these synagogue services, as they do today.

In the Jerusalem Temple

Herod, the father of Herod Antipas (see above, page 69) had built a new Temple for Jerusalem, twice as large as the one before it. The work required ten thousand builders and a thousand priests trained as masons. Begun in 19 BC, the basic structure was finished ten years later, but the builders continued to enrich it with precious stones. Only in AD 64 was the Temple completely finished. Six years later the Romans burned it to the ground.

Inside were many different rooms, approached by no fewer than eight separate gates. One courtyard was open to the Gentiles; another was reserved for women, who were not allowed to go any further inside; and there was a Temple schoolroom. At the heart of the Temple was the Holy Place, with an altar, the table of the 'shewbread' (loaves set before God) and a seven-branched lamp. A veil separated this Holy Place from the Holy of Holies, into which only the high priest was allowed to enter, and then only once a year.

A scale model of Jerusalem. The big building is the Temple

Assignments

K 1 How does Luke make it clear to us that John that the Baptist was the forerunner of Jesus?

K 2 Jesus insisted that he had come to minister to outsiders. Name some of these mentioned in Luke's gospel.

U 3 'I have not come to call the righteous, but sinners to repentance,' said Jesus. What do you think this means?

U K 4 Why do you think Jesus chose the name 'apostles' for his twelve closest disciples? What did Jesus instruct them to do?

U 5 What is your interpretation of the words, 'So therefore, whoever of you does not renounce all that he has cannot be my disciple'?

U K 6 'If any man would come after me, let him deny himself and take up his cross daily and follow me.' What is your understanding of these words of Jesus? Can you think of any people who have fulfilled this obligation?

E 7 Do you think people today truly follow Jesus?

K 8 According to Luke chapter 9, verses 51 to 55, Jesus travels through Samaria but the Samaritans refuse to give him hospitality. Why did they do this? Later in his gospel Luke speaks kindly of the Samaritans. Give an account of two such occasions.

U 9 Read the story on page 68 and work out why the association calls itself the Samaritans.

K E 10 For many of the people who lived at the time of Jesus, his demands were too great. Describe some of these demands. Do you think they are too great for us today? Give reasons to support your answer.

K U 11 What did Jesus think about the scribes? What did this group have in common with the Pharisees? In your own words write about the parable of the Pharisee and the tax collector. What do we learn from this story?

K 12 Write what you know about the following: the Samaritans; the Romans at the time of Jesus; Pontius Pilate; synagogues?

K 13 Describe the Jerusalem Temple.

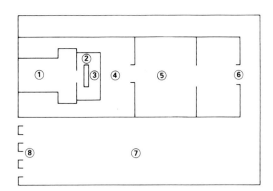

Plan of Herod's Temple in Jerusalem.

1 Holy of Holies
2 Altar
3 Court of the priests
4 Court of Jewish men

5 Court of Jewish women
6 Beautiful Gate
7 Court of non-Jews (the Gentiles)
8 Porticos

K U 14 Give some examples of how people today show their intolerance to one another. What does Luke's gospel teach about intolerance?

U K 15 Jesus asked, 'What does it profit a man if he gains the whole world and loses or forfeits himself?' (Luke chapter 9, verse 25).
　　　　(a) What do you think he meant by this?
　　　　(b) Illustrate your answer by examples, imaginary or real.

Ethiopian Jews worship in New York.

5 The teaching of Jesus

Jesus teaches by means of miracles

'It will be a miracle if Chelsea beats Manchester United next week,' football fans might say. Or someone in hospital says, 'The way I survived that train crash was a miracle.'

They don't really mean 'a miracle'. They mean that the events they are describing are in some way amazing; but no more. The proper meaning of 'miracle' is something that can only have happened by the natural laws of the universe being set aside. This is what Luke and the other gospels claim Jesus could do. In this way, they believed, he was displaying on earth the powers of God himself, who created the universe in the first place.

Here is an example:

> One day he got into a boat with his disciples, and he said to them, 'Let us go across to the other side of the lake.' So they set out, and as they sailed he fell asleep. And a storm of wind came down on the lake, and they were filling with water, and were in danger. And they went and woke him, saying, 'Master, Master, we are perishing!' And he awoke and rebuked the wind and the raging waves; and they ceased, and there was a calm. He said to them, 'Where is your faith?' And they were afraid, and they marvelled, saying to one another, 'Who is this, that he commands even the wind and water, and they obey him?'
>
> (chapter 8, verses 22 to 25)

Their question arises because Jesus is showing exactly the powers of God. As Psalm 107, verses 23 to 29, says:

> Some went down to the sea in ships,
>   doing business on great waters;
> they saw the deeds of the Lord,
>   his wondrous works in the deep.
> For he commanded and raised the stormy wind,
>   which lifted up the waves of the sea.
> They mounted up to heaven, they went down to the depths;

their courage melted away in their evil plight;
they reeled and staggered like drunken men,
 and were at their wits' end.
Then they cried to the Lord in their trouble,
 and he delivered them from their distress;
he made the storm be still,
 and the waves of the sea were hushed.

Another nature miracle

Miracles such as this one are often described as 'nature miracles',
since Jesus appears to be commanding the natural world and bending
it to his will. As we have just seen with the calming of the storm, they
are not simply displays of power. Here is a second one from Luke's
gospel:

> ... he saw two boats by the lake; but the fishermen had gone out
> of them and were washing their nets. Getting into one of the boats,
> which was Simon's, he asked him to put out a little from the land.
> And he sat down and taught the people from the boat. And when
> he had ceased speaking, he said to Simon, 'Put out into the deep
> and let down your nets for a catch.' And Simon answered, 'Master,
> we toiled all night and took nothing! But at your word I will let
> down the nets.' And when they had done this, they enclosed a
> great shoal of fish; and as their nets were breaking, they beckoned
> to their partners in the other boat to come and help them. And
> they came and filled both the boats, so that they began to sink.
> But when Simon Peter saw it, he fell down at Jesus' knees,
> saying, 'Depart from me, for I am a sinful man, O Lord.' For he
> was astonished, and all that were with him, at the catch of fish
> which they had taken; and so also were James and John, sons of
> Zebedee, who were partners with Simon. And Jesus said to Simon,
> 'Do not be afraid; henceforth you will be catching men.' And when
> they had brought their boats to land, they left everything and
> followed him.

(chapter 5, verses 2 to 11)

Again this story is not just a simple demonstration of Jesus's
extraordinary powers. Telling us about the miracle, Luke is also telling
us something about being a follower of Jesus.

First, he wants to say, like Peter we should obey Jesus's commands,
even if we think they will bring us no earthly gain. Next, we must be
prepared to leave everything to follow him. Thirdly, we shall be
amazed at how many men and women will respond to his teaching.
Finally, Jesus needs many others to help in his mission.

The miracle thus fits in with a saying of Jesus reported later in Luke's
gospel: 'He said to them, "The harvest is plentiful, but the labourers are

few; pray therefore the Lord of the harvest to send out labourers into the harvest."' (chapter 10, verse 2)

Jesus's miracles display the majesty of God

Why, when he experiences this miracle, does Peter beg Jesus to leave him because he is a sinful man? Is it because he sees that Jesus is no ordinary master. Jesus is the Lord of the universe — as the miracle has shown — and Peter is beginning to recognise this.

Once, when telling how Jesus healed a boy who suffered terrible convulsions, Luke ends his account of the miracle not by telling us that the onlookers were amazed at Jesus's power. Instead he reports that 'all were astonished at the majesty of God' (chapter 9, verse 43). The power of God working through Jesus is being displayed in his miracles.

Beelzebul versus the finger of God

Jesus's enemies refused to believe this. They claimed that he was using stronger demons to cast out weaker ones. Jesus, they said, was a follower of the prince of demons, Beelzebul.

The notion, Jesus replied, was absurd. Why should the devil, Satan, fight against his own forces? Jesus's own conquest of these demons showed that God was already beginning his rule in the world. 'If it is by the finger of God that I cast out demons,' he claimed, 'then the kingdom of God has come upon you.' (chapter 11, verses 14 to 23)

A taste of the heavenly banquet

Near a city called Bethsaida Jesus attracted a huge crowd of about five thousand men. He welcomed them, taught them about the kingdom of God and healed those who were sick.

The crowd was still there when evening came, and Jesus's disciples asked him to send them away to find lodgings and food. Jesus answered, 'You give them something to eat.' The disciples replied, 'We have no more than five loaves and two fish.' Jesus said, 'Make them all sit down.'

The five thousand did so, in groups of about fifty. Then Jesus took the five loaves and the two fish, looked up to heaven, and blessed and broke them. He gave the food to the disciples, who set it before the crowd. Luke declares that 'all ate and were satisfied. And they took up what was left over, twelve baskets in all.' (chapter 9, verses 10 to 18)

Did this really happen? Some people have argued that it was a kind of early Mass or Holy Communion. This is the act of worship when Christians take a small piece of bread and a sip of wine, as Jesus told them to do. Jesus's action in looking to heaven and asking God's blessing on the loaves and fish would fit in with this, even though what he was doing here was also a normal Jewish way of asking God to bless food. He told his followers to do this over bread and over wine at their acts of worship. And the detail that twelve baskets were left over could mean that his twelve disciples would later preside over such meals.

But even if everyone took a small piece of bread or fish, five loaves and two fish could not have been enough for five thousand people, leaving aside the twelve basketfuls left over.

Once we accept the story as Luke tells it, we begin to see deeper into its meaning. First, it would remind all the Jews present of the time when Moses was leading their forefathers through the wilderness. When they ran out of food, God fed them. And there was sometimes some left. (Exodus chapter 16, verses 4 to 6). Jesus is once again displaying the same powers as God.

Secondly, as Luke told his readers, Jesus promised that in the kingdom of God, 'men will come from east and west, and from north and south, and sit at table' (chapter 13, verse 29). The prophets looked forward to feasting with God when all earthly evils are ended and God alone rules. As Isaiah put it:

> ... the Lord of hosts will make for all peoples a feast of fat things, a feast of wine on the lees, of fat things full of marrow, of wine on the lees well refined .... He will swallow up death for ever, and the Lord God will wipe away tears from all faces, and the reproach of his people he will take away from all the earth.'
>
> (Isaiah chapter 25, verses 6 and 8)

In feeding the huge crowd at Bethsaida, Jesus was giving his followers a foretaste of that heavenly banquet.

The miracle of feeding five thousand is thus not designed simply as a demonstration of Jesus's power. It is another teaching miracle, showing Jesus as one who, like Moses, leads his people from despair and danger to safety; as one who displays divine powers; and as the one who will preside over the heavenly feast in the kingdom of God.

Lord over death

'The Lord God will swallow up death for ever,' Isaiah promised. We have already seen that Luke believed Jesus had brought back from death the son of a widow at Nain (pages 9–10). Only Luke's gospel tells us this story.

Another astonishing miracle story we have so far simply touched on is also described in Matthew's gospel and Mark's gospel. This is the account of how Jesus brought back to life the daughter of the ruler of the synagogue named Jairus (chapter 8, verses 40 to 56).

Once more Jesus's disciples are being taught far more than merely that he is endowed with the powers which normally we associate only with God himself. Here Luke also wants to teach us that faith in Jesus is vital if his powers are to be released into the world.

Luke tells us that when Jesus finally arrived at Jairus's house and found the girl dead, people laughed at his claims that she might be raised again. He therefore allowed only Jairus, Jairus's wife and his three closest disciples into the room where the girl lay dead. They at least had faith in him.

Then he took her by the hand, said, 'Child, arise,' and — Luke records — 'her spirit returned, and she got up at once.'

Faith and miracles

It is easier to see the role of faith when Jesus was performing miracles of healing, rather than these astonishing acts of raising people from death and controlling nature. We know that our own minds can often have a remarkable control over our bodies.

If we are relaxed, our bodies often respond positively. If we are mentally tense, our bodies become tense too. A newspaper recently reported on 'Relaxation exercises that can help cancer patients.'

RELAXATION exercises are proving to be helpful for women who are having radiotherapy treatment for breast cancer. The same exercises could also be helpful for many other people with different types of cancer or other stressful diseases.

Evidence for a link between life stresses, such as bereavement or separation, and cancer is not yet convincing. Nevertheless, doctors who looked at the lives of cancer patients have become more aware of the stress caused by the disease itself. Cancer patients not only suffer the fatigue and debility caused by treatment, they also face an uncertain future in which they may lose their position in life.

(Independent, 8 November 1988)

Our own mental state can sometimes affect our physical state. So, faith may well do so.

Yet in the miracle we have just looked at, it is not the dead girl's faith but the faith of others that Jesus calls on. They have faith that Jesus is Lord both over life and over death.

Healing a leper

Sometimes sick people came to Jesus, confident that he could heal them if he wished. One such person was a leper.

Leprosy has remained a dreaded disease in some parts of the world well into the twentieth century. Unless it is treated in time, the sick person's fingers drop off. White patches appear on the sufferer's skin, as well as grotesque disfiguration and huge ugly sores.

Since the disease is contagious, in Jesus's day lepers were a perfect example of 'untouchables'. By law they had to live outside towns and cities. They were ordered to shout, wherever they went, 'Unclean, unclean.'

One of them approached Jesus with the words, 'Lord, if you will, you can make me clean.' Jesus stretched out his hand and touched the untouchable. 'And immediately,' says Luke, 'the leprosy left him.'

Mark's gospel, in telling this story, stresses Jesus's compassion. Luke leaves this out. For him the miracle, although it obviously does illustrate this aspect of Jesus's character, is above all one about faith.

The faith of a blind beggar

Compassion for the blind also obviously moved Jesus, as it still moves many people today.

But when Jesus cured a blind man near Jericho, it was again the faith of the man which was all-important. The man cried out, 'Jesus, Son of David, have mercy on me.' As he healed the man, Jesus said to him, 'Receive your sight; your faith has made you well.' (chapter 18, verses 35 to 43)

The importance of faith is stressed again when Jesus heals a boy whose sickness makes him foam at the mouth and suffer convulsions. His father has appealed to the disciples to heal his son, but they have failed. As Jesus heals the boy, he asks his followers, 'O faithless and perverse generation, how long am I to be with you and bear with you?' (chapter 9, verses 37 to 43)

Jesus heals the mentally ill

At the time of Jesus, anyone who was mentally ill was considered to be in the grip of the devil or the devil's servants, who were known as demons. From the description of a sick man in chapter 4, verses 33 to 37, people seemed to think too that anyone suffering epileptic fits had also been taken over by such a demon.

Several times in Luke's gospel we find Jesus curing these unhappy people. Luke describes such healings as if Jesus is commanding the demons to leave the sick person. (chapter 4, verses 40f)

Once, Luke tells us, Jesus allowed the demons to leave a sick man and enter instead a herd of pigs — which immediately went mad, rushed over a cliff into a lake, and were drowned. (chapter 8, verses 26 to 33)

Compassion and the miracles of Jesus

Alongside the deeper meaning in all these miracles, the element of compassion must not be forgotten. One sabbath Jesus was teaching in a synagogue when he saw a crippled woman who had not been able to straighten up for eighteen years. She had not asked him for help, but 'Jesus called to her and said, "Woman, you are freed from your infirmity." He laid his hands on her; immediately she was made straight; and she praised God.' (chapter 13, verses 10 to 13)

We would not know of this miracle (which does not occur in any other gospel) save that Luke puts it into his gospel because he wants to tell us how the ruler of the synagogue became angry because Jesus healed on a sabbath day. But it shows Jesus's spontaneous kindness.

These young dancers being taught by a member of the Royal Ballet Company are all blind.

Do we offer the disabled in our own society such compassion? Read this newspaper article:

Lack of support 'imprisons' disabled at home

Three-quarters of Britain's young severely disabled people are imprisoned at home with no hope of living independent lives.

Some have to wait for up to two years for equipment to be provided or adaptations to be made, according to a report published yesterday by the Prince of Wales Advisory Group on Disability.

Even special housing schemes fail, it says. One young man who moved from an institution to a supported housing association flat has already waited 16 months for kitchen units to be lowered and bed bar and bath rail to be fitted. 'He currently needs help for almost all his personal needs but if these adaptations were carried out he would be almost entirely self-sufficient,' *Living Options Lottery*, a two-year study of provision for the young disabled, says.

The report found services for the disabled were 'scarce, patchily distributed and a low priority among service providers'.

(*Independent*, 9 December 1988)

A physical handicap does not mean helplessness.

The central meaning of Jesus's miracles

John the Baptist, Luke says, sent two of his followers to Jesus to ask him whether he was the long-expected Christ or not (chapter 7, verse 18).

Jesus answered him by referring to the prophet Isaiah's description of all the good things that would happen when the whole earth accepts God's rule:

> Then the eyes of the blind shall be opened,
>   and the ears of the deaf unstopped;
> then shall the lame man leap like a hart,
>   and the tongue of the dumb sing for joy.
>
> (Isaiah chapter 35, verses 5f)

In another passage Isaiah wrote:

> In that day the deaf shall hear
>   the words of a book
> and out of gloom and darkness
>   the eyes of the blind shall see.
> The meek shall obtain fresh joy in the Lord,
>   and the poor among men shall exult in the Holy One of Israel.
>
> (Isaiah chapter 29, verses 18f)

All these things, as John and his followers could see for themselves, were already happening in Jesus's ministry.

Jesus therefore replied to John's disciples, 'Go and tell John what you have seen and heard: the blind receive their sight, the lame walk, lepers are cleansed, the deaf hear, the dead are raised up, the poor have the good news preached to them. And blessed is he who takes no offence at me.'

In effect, his miracles are demonstrating the truth that he is the Christ, the Holy One of Israel, who has come to bring about God's kingdom on earth. (chapter 7, verses 22f)

Teaching in parables

Jesus had the gift of telling brilliant short stories to illustrate his teaching. Such stories, or parables, were used a lot by Jewish teachers in Jesus's time. 'Parable ' is a word which means to compare two similar things with each other. Jesus would seize on everyday events, sharpen their point and use them to open people's eyes to what he was teaching them.

The blind leading the blind

Here is one of his shortest parables, warning his followers not to heed false teachers:

> Can a blind man lead a blind man? Will they not both fall into a pit?
> (chapter 6, verse 39)

Taking a speck from your brother's eye

A moment later Luke shows him comparing the hypocrite to someone trying to take a speck out of his brother's eye when a log is blinding his own. 'You hypocrite,' Jesus comments, 'first take the log out of your own eye, and then you will see clearly to take out the speck that is in your brother's eye.' (chapter 6, verses 41f)

Here is a twentieth-century British example of a group of people doing precisely what Jesus advised:

The party is over for worried police at Christmas

Many Scotland Yard detectives have axed their Christmas parties – because of fears they will be raided by police.

Half the CID's seasonal get-togethers throughout the Metropolitan Police area have been cancelled following a purge against possible bribery.

Police party organisers have been told by senior officers they must show receipts for all drinks and food and cannot accept any gifts.

(*Daily Mail*, 30 November 1988)

Parables found only in Luke

Not every parable told by Jesus is as short and pithy as these two. But almost every one of them makes a single point, sharply and clearly. Jesus obviously told countless such stories. Some of them we know only from Luke's gospel.

The fact that Luke chose to tell us these particular parables shows his own special insights into Jesus and his gospel. For instance, as we have already seen, Luke's Jesus teaches us that God is always ready to give sinners a second chance. The parables of **the lost coin** and **the prodigal son** (chapter 15, verses 8 to 32) movingly illustrate this.

Luke adds these two parables after another famous story, the parable of **the lost sheep**, Jesus's response when 'the tax collectors and sinners were all drawing near to him' and 'the Pharisees and the scribes murmured, saying, "This man receives sinners and eats with them."' According to Luke, Jesus then asked:

> What man of you, having a hundred sheep, if he has lost one of them, does not leave the ninety-nine in the wilderness, and go after the one which is lost, until he finds it? And when he comes home he calls together his friends and neighbours, saying to them, 'Rejoice with me, for I have found my sheep which was lost.'

Jesus explains this parable with the words, 'Just so, I tell you, there is more joy in heaven over one sinner who repents than over ninety-nine righteous persons who need no repentance.' (chapter 15, verses 3 to 7)

Matthew too tells the same parable, but he gives it an entirely different meaning from Luke's. In Matthew's gospel the story is used to illustrate God's care for children. When he has told the parable, Jesus says, according to Matthew, 'So it is not the will of my Father who is in heaven that one of these little ones should perish.' (Matthew chapter 18, verses 10 to 14)

Luke's version thus tells us much about his own special concerns — Jesus's love for sinners and outsiders, God's willingness to give us a second chance.

Everyday parallels

Jesus's parable of the lost sheep reveals his skill at taking ordinary countryside happenings and filling them with meaning about his mission and God's love. He does the same when he urges his disciples to take comfort from **the ravens** and **the lilies**.

The ravens are fed by God even though they have no storehouses or barns. The lilies neither sew nor toil nor spin, but, said Jesus, referring to the Jews' richest ever king, 'even Solomon in all his glory was not arrayed like one of these.'

The disciples, he pointed out, are more important than either ravens or lilies. God will see to their necessary food and clothing. (chapter 12, verses 22 to 28)

An acted parable

Once Jesus settled an argument among his disciples as to which of them was the greatest by setting a child next to them. He said, 'Whoever receives this child in my name receives me, and whoever receives me receives him who sent me; for he who is least among you all is the one who is great.' (chapter 9, verses 46 to 48)

Instead of telling a parable of a child to illustrate the humility required by a disciple, he brought on stage a real child and acted his parable.

'Whoever receives this child in my name receives me.' Have we yet started to take Jesus's statement seriously? In 1988 the Children's Society declared:

Some 75,000 children and young people go missing every year, yet nobody knows who they all are or where they come from. The only estimate of the size of the problem comes from a survey of chief constables, carried out by The Children's Society, a leading charity that is calling for changes in the law to help the young runaways who are at risk on our streets.

(*Church Times,* 9 December 1988)

The good Samaritan

One parable told to us only by Luke shows us his own and his master's compassion, as well as their love for the outsider (for the hero is a Samaritan, see above, page 68) and their belief that many religious leaders had forgotten their true calling.

A lawyer asked Jesus what he should do to inherit eternal life. Jesus threw the question back to him, and the lawyer answered, 'You shall love the Lord your God with all your heart and with all your soul and with all your strength and with all your mind; and your neighbour as yourself.' Jesus said, 'You have answered right; do this, and you shall live.

But the lawyer wanted more from Jesus. He asked, 'Who is my neighbour?' Jesus's answer was the parable of **the good Samaritan**:

> A man was going down from Jerusalem to Jericho, and he fell among robbers, who stripped him and beat him, and departed, leaving him half dead. Now by chance a priest was going down that road; and when he saw him he passed by on the other side. So likewise a Levite, when he came to the place and saw him passed by on the other side. But a Samaritan, as he journeyed, came to where he was; and when he saw him, he had compassion, and went to him and bound up his wounds, pouring on oil and wine; then he set him on his own beast and brought him to an inn, and took care of him. And the next day he took out two denarii and gave them to the innkeeper, saying, 'Take care of him; and whatever more you spend, I will repay you when I come back.'

Jesus asked the lawyer which of the three had proved a neighbour to the man who fell among the robbers. The lawyer replied, 'The one who showed mercy on him.' Jesus answered, 'Go and do likewise.' (chapter 10, verses 25 to 37)

Does anyone really behave like the priest and the Levite in Jesus's parable? Read the following report from the *Daily Telegraph*, 16 November 1988:

Girl hit by 20 cars on motorway

A 12-year-old girl was run over by at least 20 cars when she tried to wave down drivers to save her dying father after a French motorway accident.

Gaelle Gombert was killed as she and her sisters, aged six and three, tried to find help for their father, badly injured when his car overturned. None of the vehicles stopped after running over Gaelle.

The accident happened on a slip road of the A4 Quincy-Voisin, south-east of Paris, on Sunday.

Allegories

Sometimes what the gospels call parables would be better called 'allegories'. Whereas a parable has one main point, and the details are there only to sharpen that point, in an allegory the details need explaining too.

Teaching in Jerusalem as his arrest and trial drew near, Jesus told such a parable/allegory about **a vineyard**:

> A man planted a vineyard, and let it out to tenants, and went into another country for a long while. When the time came, he sent a servant to the tenants, that they should give him some of the fruit of the vineyard; but the tenants beat him, and sent him away empty-handed. And he sent another servant; him also they beat and treated shamefully, and sent him away empty-handed. And he sent yet a third; this one they wounded and cast out. Then the owner of the vineyard said, 'What shall I do? I will send my beloved son; it may be they will respect him.' But when the tenants saw him, they said to themselves, 'This is the heir; let us kill him, that the inheritance may be ours.' And they cast him out of the vineyard and killed him. What then will the owner of the vineyard do to them? He will come and destroy those tenants, and give the vineyard to others.
>
> (chapter 20, verses 9 to 16)

As Jesus's hearers listened to this allegory they would instantly identify the vineyard as Israel, for this they knew was an idea found in the prophet Isaiah (chapter 5, verses 1 to 7).

The landlord was clearly God, and the servants represented the prophets whose words had been repeatedly neglected by many and who had often been treated shamefully. The son was Jesus himself. Those religious and other leaders of the Jews who were soon to kill him recognised that he was telling this parable against them.

A second allegory, this one found only in Luke's gospel, seems to have been composed out of various pieces of Jesus's teaching to describe the life of the early Church. It describes **waiting servants**:

> Let your loins be girded and your lamps burning, and be like men who are waiting for their master to come home from the marriage feast, so that they may open to him at once when he comes and knocks. Blessed are those servants whom the master finds awake when he comes; truly, I say to you, he will gird himself and have them sit at table, and he will come and serve them. If he comes in the second watch, or in the third, and finds them so, blessed are those servants! But know this, that if the householder had known at what hour the thief was coming, he would not have left his house to

be broken into. You must also be ready; for the Son of man is coming at an unexpected hour.

(chapter 12, verses 35 to 40)

The waiting servants probably stand for the early Church. Jesus is the absent master. The master's return represents his coming again in glory.

The parable/allegory of **the sower** proved so difficult for Jesus's disciples that Luke tells us he had to interpret it for them himself.

A sower went out to sow his seed; and as he sowed, some fell along the path, and was trodden under foot, and the birds of the air devoured it. And some fell on the rock; and as it grew up, it withered away, because it had no moisture. And some fell among thorns; and the thorns grew with it and choked it. And some fell into good soil and grew, and yielded a hundredfold.'

(chapter 8, verses 5 to 8)

Luke calls this a parable. Even so, when the disciples ask Jesus to explain it, he does so as if it were an allegory. Every detail has its corresponding equivalent in real life:

The seed is the word of God. The ones along the path are those who have heard; then the devil comes and takes away the word from their hearts, that they may not believe and be saved. And the ones on the rock are those who, when they hear the word, receive it with joy; but these have no root; they believe for a while and in time of temptation fall away. And as for what fell among the thorns, they are those who hear, but as they go on their way they are choked by the cares and riches and pleasures of life, and their fruit does not mature. And as for that in the good soil, they are those who, hearing the word, hold it fast in an honest and good heart, and bring forth fruit with patience.

(chapter 8, verses 11 to 15)

Sayings

Often Jesus simply expressed part of his teaching in a short, unforgettable saying which was neither a parable nor an allegory. When he had told the parable/allegory of the vineyard which we read a moment ago, his hearers cried, 'God forbid.'

Jesus then quoted Psalm 118, verse 22: 'The very stone which the builders rejected has become head of the corner.' Obviously he was applying this to himself, soon to be rejected by men but raised to glory by God.

He then added a powerful saying expressing his own powers of judgement over evil ones:

> Every one who falls on that stone will be broken to pieces; but when it falls on any one it will crush him.
>
> (chapter 20, verses 18f)

Conflict, judgment and promise

Such striking sayings occur repeatedly in Luke's gospel. Earlier in the gospel Jesus suddenly cries out, 'I came to cast fire upon the earth; and would that it were already kindled!' (chapter 12, verse 49) — another reference to his coming as judge.

Jesus knew in one sense that this judgement was already happening. His presence divided people into those who passionately supported him and those who equally passionately turned against him. He expected even close families to be divided: 'Do you think that I have come to give peace on earth? No, I tell you, but rather division.' (chapter 12, verse 51)

This is a startling remark from one who has told us to love our enemies. But not all of Jesus's sayings are about judgement or conflict. When, for instance, Jesus was warning his followers of the sacrifices they must make, he suddenly said, 'Fear not, little flock, for it is your Father's good pleasure to give you the kingdom.' (chapter 12, verse 32)

Sayings and parables

Often these sayings are backed up by parables. Jesus illustrated the conflict between the old and the new by observing:

> No one tears a piece from a new garment and puts it on an old garment; if he does, he will tear the new, and the piece from the new will not match the old. And no one puts new wine into old wineskins; if he does, the new wine will burst the skins and it will be spilled, and the skins will be destroyed. But new wine must be put into fresh wineskins.

At first sight these two parables might seem to be condemning the old Jewish religion and putting in its place Christianity. But as we have already seen, Luke does not share the bitterness towards Jews expressed at times in Matthew's gospel. His passage goes on:

> And no one after drinking old wine desires new; for he says, 'The old is good.'
>
> (chapter 5, verses 36 to 39)

The new versus the old

Luke remains faithful to Jesus's own view that the teachings of the

Jewish law and the Jewish prophets remain sacred, in spite of the new teachings of Jesus.

This does not mean that the coming of Jesus had made no difference. Luke puts two of Jesus's sayings one after the other. They make it clear that the relationship between the old teachings and Jesus's new message was a difficult one:

chapter 16, verse 16
The law and the prophets were until John; since then the good news of the kingdom of God is preached, and everyone enters it violently.

chapter 16, verse 17
But it is easier for heaven and earth to pass away, than for one dot of the law to become void.

Wandering sayings

These loose sayings were obviously collected by the gospel writers and put into their text wherever they thought best for that text. The sayings seem to have been on many people's lips, without anyone really knowing when Jesus actually said them.

Take a saying that stands by itself in Luke's gospel (chapter 10, verse 16):

> He who hears you hears me, and he who rejects you rejects me, and he who rejects me rejects him who sent me.

Look it up in Matthew chapter 10, verse 40, and you find the saying standing at a totally different place in the gospel.

Another 'wandering saying' of Jesus recorded by Luke runs, 'some are last who will be first, and some are first who will be last' (chapter 13, verse 30). Both Mark and Matthew in their gospels put the saying in a different place from Luke. (See Mark chapter 10, verse 31; Matthew chapter 19, verse 30.)

Parables of the kingdom of God

When Jesus's disciples asked him the meaning of the difficult parable/allegory of the sower, he said, 'To you it has been given to know the secrets of the kingdom of God; but for others they are in parables, so that seeing they may not see, and hearing they may not understand.' (chapter 8, verses 9f)

It is, however, interesting to compare the explanation of this allegory in Luke with the ones given in Mark (chapter 4, verses 14 to 20) and Matthew (chapter 13, verses 19 to 23). Both explanations differ from each other and from that given in Luke.

This has led some people to conclude that the story of the sower was at first a straightforward parable, with one point to make, and not an allegory.

What was that point? In the explanations of both Mark and Matthew the ones who do hear the word of God and accept it are said to 'bear fruit, thirtyfold and sixtyfold and a hundredfold'. It is likely that here is the clue. Jesus was telling a parable about the way God spreads his word everywhere and on everyone, so that in time, no matter how many people reject it, his kingdom is bound to flourish amazingly.

Another parable of the kingdom in Luke seems to confirm this. Jesus said:

> What is the kingdom of God like? And to what shall I compare it? It is like a grain of mustard seed which a man took and sowed in his garden; and it grew and became a tree, and the birds of the air made nests in its branches.
>
> (chapter 13, verses 18f)

No doubt the band of disciples is tiny, virtually hidden in the ground. But the seed has been sown, and ultimately will blossom abundantly.

Immediately after this, Luke gives another of Jesus's parables of the kingdom, this time comparing it with another substance which, though hidden like the mustard seed, is busy at work. The kingdom of God, he says, 'is like leaven which a woman took and hid in three measures of flour till it was all leavened' (chapter 13, verses 20f).

Seek the kingdom above all things

'Do not seek what you are to eat and what you are to drink, nor be of anxious mind,' Jesus said to his disciples. 'For all the nations of the world seek these things; and your Father knows that you need them. Instead seek his kingdom, and these things shall be yours as well.' (chapter 12, verses 29f)

Jesus admitted that his demands were great, but they represented the only way to a place in God's kingdom. 'Strive to enter by the narrow door,' he once warned the disciples, 'for many, I tell you, will seek to enter and will not be able.' He went on to describe the plight of 'workers of iniquity' knocking on a house door and being refused entrance by the householder. Instead others will be welcome, from north, south, east and west, to sit down at table in the kingdom of God. (chapter 13, verses 23 to 30)

The great banquet

Jesus ended this parable of **the householder and the workers of iniquity** with the words, 'And behold, some are last who will be first, and some are first who will be last.'

The notion of a heavenly banquet at which God will welcome the utterly unexpected and reject those who imagined themselves to be certain of a place next appears in a parable Jesus told when someone said to him, 'Blessed is he who shall eat bread in the kingdom of God!'

Jesus immediately told a parable of a man who gave **a great banquet.** None of those the invited came, everyone of them offering an excuse. In response the man ordered his servant, 'Go out quickly to the streets and lanes of the city, and bring in the poor and maimed, blind and lame.' When that was done there was still room for more, so the man sent his servant to the highways and hedges to compel more to come in. 'For I tell you,' he said, 'none of those men who were invited shall taste my banquet.' (chapter 14, verses 15 to 24)

As well as a clear hint of the rejection of those religious and political leaders who were to condemn Jesus, here is another example of how Luke (who alone tells us the parable in this form) shows us Jesus's care for the outcast, downtrodden, unfortunate and poor.

The kingdom of God and this world

Jesus also suggests in another parable which we find only in Luke that the picture of the kingdom of God shown in the story above ought to govern our daily lives now.

To a man who had invited him to dinner Jesus said, 'When you give a

Volunteers help provide food and good cheer to the homeless at Christmas.

dinner or a banquet, do not invite your friends or your brothers or your kinsmen or rich neighbours, lest they also invite you in return, and you be repaid. But when you give a feast, invite the poor, the maimed, the lame, the blind, and you will be blessed, because they cannot repay you. You will be repaid at the resurrection of the just.' (chapter 14, verses 12 to 14)

The kingdom and Jesus's second coming

Although Luke clearly believed that the kingdom of God was already at work in the world, by the time he wrote his gospel most Christians had abandoned Mark's view that Jesus would return almost immediately to set up God's kingdom completely.

Luke faithfully reports Jesus's saying, 'I tell you truly, there are some standing here who will not taste death before they see the kingdom of God (chapter 9, verse 27). Yet you can see him toning down this notion if you compare the following two passages.

Mark chapter 13, verses 32 to 37
But of that day or that hour no one knows, not even the angels in heaven, nor the Son, but only the Father. Take heed, watch; for you do not know when the time will come. It is like a man going on a journey, when he leaves home and puts his servants in charge, each with his work, and commands the doorkeeper to be on the watch. Watch therefore — for you do not know when the master of the house will come, in the evening, or at midnight, or at cockcrow, or in the morning — lest he come suddenly and find you asleep. And what I say to you I say to all: Watch.

Luke chapter 21, verses 34 to 36
But take heed to yourselves lest your hearts be weighed down with dissipation and drunkenness and cares of this life, and that day come upon you suddenly like a snare; for it will come upon all who dwell upon the face of the whole earth. But watch at all times, praying that you may have strength to escape all these things that will take place, and to stand before the Son of man.'

Jesus even told a parable, Luke says, 'because he was near to Jerusalem and because people supposed that the kingdom of God was to appear immediately' (chapter 19, verses 11 to 27). The parable, oddly enough, does not seem to deal with the question, which makes it all the more certain that *Luke* rather than Jesus was the one who wished to insist that the kingdom of God will not necessarily arrive instantly

The kingdom of God is near

Even so, Luke shows us that Jesus insisted the kingdom of God was near, quite apart from his second coming. When he sent out his seventy missionaries, part of their message was to announce in every town, 'The kingdom of God has come near to you.' (chapter 10, verses 9 and 11)

Later he was asked by the Pharisees when the kingdom of God was coming. He replied, 'The kingdom of God is not coming with signs to be observed; nor will they say, "Lo, here it is!" or "There!" for behold, the kingdom of God is in the midst of you.' (chapter 17, verses 20f)

This is entirely in accord with his parable which describes the kingdom as leaven, working in dough.

Jesus himself believed that he had brought the kingdom of God near. The divisions he caused and the judgement he brought anticipated what would happen when the kingdom finally came. 'In that night there will be two in one bed; and one will be taken and the other left,' he said. 'There will be two women grinding together; one will be taken and the other left.' (chapter 17, verses 34f)

Even his praise of children and their humility was connected with the kingdom of God. At one time, Luke says, 'they were bringing children to him that he might touch them; and when the disciples saw it, they rebuked them. But Jesus called them to him, saying, "Let the children come to me, and do not hinder them; for to such belongs the kingdom of God. Truly, I say to you, whoever does not receive the kingdom of God like a child shall not enter it.' (chapter 18, verses 15 to 17)

When he urged his disciples to have the humility of children, Jesus was preaching on earth the laws of the kingdom.

The kingdom and the Church

As we have seen, Luke is the only gospel writer to have produced a sequel to his gospel. In the Acts of the Apostles he shows that it is now the task of the earliest Church to preach the kingdom of God to the ends of the earth.

For this reason Luke stresses that the same Holy Spirit which inspired Jesus inspires his followers. At the beginning of Jesus's ministry, Luke tells us, 'Jesus returned in the power of the Spirit into Galilee'. Later on he told his disciples that if evil parents still give good presents to their children, 'how much more will the heavenly Father give the Holy Spirit to those who ask him!'

Finally, at the beginning of the Acts of the Apostles, Luke tells us that this Holy Spirit was poured out on Jesus's followers as they began their

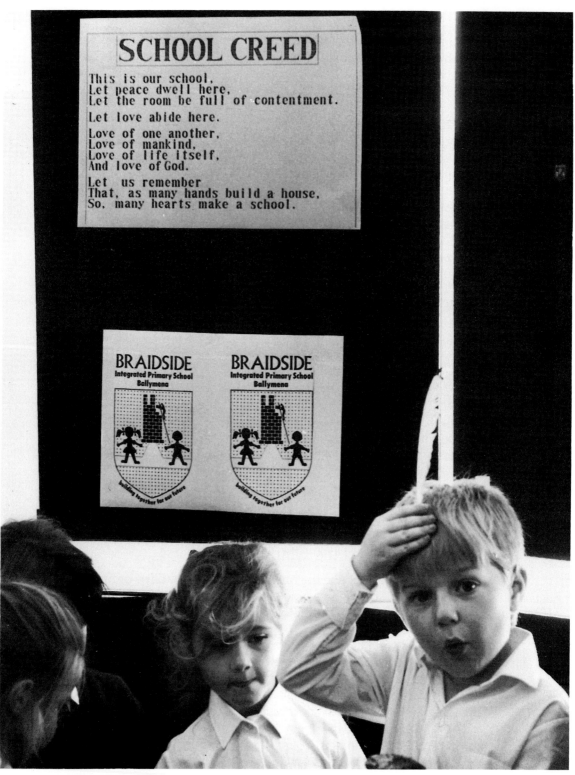

This integrated school in Northern Ireland has a creed about living together in peace.
Integrated schools educate Catholic and Protestant children side by side.

great work on behalf of the kingdom of God. It is now the Church's task to preach the kingdom of God from Jerusalem throughout the world. (Luke chapter 4, verse 14 and chapter 11, verse 13; Acts of the Apostles chapter 2, verses 1 to 3)

Beatitudes and woes

Because the laws of the kingdom of God are far removed from those of the sinful world, when Jesus began to speak about who was 'blessed' his words seemed extremely strange.

The blessed

> Blessed are you poor, for yours is the kingdom of God.
> Blessed are you that hunger now, for you shall be satisfied.
> Blessed are you that weep now, for you shall laugh.
> Blessed are you when men hate you, and when they exclude you and revile you, and cast out your name as evil, on account of the Son of man! Rejoice in that day, and leap for joy, for behold, your reward is great in heaven; for so their fathers did to the prophets.
>
> (chapter 6, verses 20 to 23)

Woes

Jesus's sermon, turning topsy-turvy the normal view of the world, continued:

> But woe to you that are rich, for you have received your consolation.
> Woe to you that are full now, for you shall hunger.
> Woe to you that laugh now, for you shall mourn and weep.
> Woe to you, when all men speak well of you, for so their fathers did to the false prophets.
>
> (chapter 6, verses 24 to 26)

No limits to love

He went on:

> Love your enemies, do good to those who hate you, bless those who curse you, pray for those who abuse you. To him who strikes you on the cheek, offer the other also; and from him who takes away your coat, do not withhold even your shirt. Give to every one who begs from you; and of him who takes away your goods, do not ask them again. And as you wish that men would do to you, do so to them.
>
> (chapter 6, verses 27 to 31)

How can anyone pray for his enemies? Here is such a prayer, written by the American religious writer Reinhold Niebuhr:

> We pray for the victims of tyranny, that they may resist oppression with courage. We pray for wicked and cruel men, whose arrogance reveals to us what the sin of our own hearts is like when it has conceived and brought forth its final fruit. We pray for ourselves who live in peace and quietness, that we may not regard our good fortune as the proof of our virtue, or rest content to have our ease at the price of other men's sorrow and tribulation.

The merciful sons of the Most High

As Jesus pointed out:

> If you love those who love you, what credit is that to you? For even sinners love those who love them. And if you do good to those who do good to you, what credit is that to you? For even sinners do the same. And if you lend to those from whom you hope to receive, what credit is that to you? Even sinners lend to sinners, to receive as much again.
>
> But love your enemies, and do good, and lend, expecting nothing in return; and your reward will be great, and you will be sons of the Most High; for he is kind to the ungrateful and the selfish. Be merciful, even as your Father is merciful.
>
> (chapter 6, verses 32 to 36)

Assignments

U 1 What do you understand by the word 'miracle'?

K U 2 Write an account of two nature miracles found in Luke's gospel. These stories are not just simple demonstrations of Jesus's extraordinary powers; they have deeper meanings. What is Luke teaching us in the two nature miracles you have retold?

K 3 'And taking the five loaves and the two fish he looked up to heaven, and blessed and broke them and gave them to the disciples to set before the crowd.' Some people have argued that this was a kind of early Christian Mass or Holy Communion. What are the similarities?

U 4 Jesus said, 'I tell you, not even in Israel have I found such faith.' Read Luke chapter 7, verses 1 to 10 and say why the centurion's faith was so exceptional.

K U 5 Tell in your own words the story of how Jesus raised from death the son of the widow of Nain. What do we learn in Luke's account of the compassion of Jesus? This miracle story contains the first occasion on which Luke refers to Jesus as 'Lord'. Why do you think he does so in this instance?

K U 6 Two public officials came to Jesus to ask him to heal someone. Who are they and what did they want Jesus to do? Why did other people laugh at Jesus?

K 7 How does the Church today continue Jesus's healing work?

K U 8 'Lord, if you will, you can make me clean.' Who said this, and what does his remark and the story connected with it illustrate?

K U 9 Give two examples from Luke's gospel of Jesus healing the mentally ill. How did the people of Jesus's time regard people who were mentally ill?

E 10 Jesus showed compassion when he healed a crippled woman on the sabbath. Do you think that in today's society we care enough for the crippled? What more could be done to help them?

U 11 What do the miracle stories in Luke's gospel tell us about Jesus?

U 12 What do you understand by the word 'parable'?

K 13 'God is always ready to give sinners a second chance.' Relate two parables from Luke's gospel to support this claim.

K E 14 By referring to three parables in Luke's gospel try to illustrate what you know about God's attitude to sinful people. What relevance does this have for us today?

K U 15 What is an allegory? Read Luke chapter 20, verses 9 to 16. What imagery is used here and what do you learn from this story?

16 'Who then is this, that he commands even wind and water, and they obey him?' (Luke chapter 8, verse 25)
K   (a) Describe the circumstances in which Jesus's disciples asked this question.
U   (b) What answer does Luke expect us to give?
E   (c) Why?

17 Jesus said, 'If it is by the finger of God that I cast out demons, then the kingdom of God has come upon you.' (chapter 11, verse 20)
K   (a) When did Jesus say this?
K   (b) Give one example of Jesus 'casting out demons', or a demon, as told in Luke's gospel.
U   (c) What do you today understand by the word 'demons' as they appear in some of the miracle stories told by Luke?

18 'Jesus answered John's disciples, "Go and tell John what you have seen and heard: the blind receive their sight, the lame walk, lepers are cleansed, and the deaf hear, the dead are raised up, the poor have the good news preached to them. And blessed is he who takes no offence at me."' (chapter 18, verses 22f)
K   (a) What question from John the Baptist prompted this reply?
K   (b) Which Old Testament prophet was Jesus quoting?
K   (c) Describe one example of the events Jesus says are happening.
U   (d) What does his answer mean about himself?

K **E** 19 Read Luke chapter 10, verses 25 to 37. From newspapers collect examples of people who still behave like the robbers. Try to find examples of the priest who passed by on the other side. Then try to find the 'good Samaritans' in our present-day world, like Valerie Taylor below. Do you think there are many?

Valerie Talyor is a physiotherapist who, for the past 21 years, has given up a comfortable life in Britain to help thousands of paralysed people in India. She has adopted two Bengali children with cerebral palsy.

20　'Just so, I tell you, there will be more joy in heaven over one sinner who repents than over ninety-nine righteous persons who need no repentance.' (chapter 15, verse 7)

(a)　Tell in your own words the parable Jesus has just told.

(b)　In what way does Luke's version of the parable differ from Matthew's version?

(c)　What does it reveal to us about Luke's special concerns?

21　Read the two following passages:

But of that day or that hour no one knows, not even the angels in heaven, nor the Son, but only the Father. Take heed, watch; for you do not know when the time will come. It is like a man going on a journey, when he leaves home and puts his servants in charge, each with his work, and commands the doorkeeper to be on the watch. Watch therefore — for you do not know when the master of the house will come, in the evening, or at midnight, or at cockcrow, or in the morning — lest he come suddenly and find you asleep. And what I say to you I say to all: Watch.
(Mark chapter 13, verses 32 to 37)

But take heed to yourselves lest your hearts be weighed down with dissipation and drunkenness and cares of this life, and that day come upon you suddenly like a snare; for it will come upon all who dwell upon the face of the whole earth. But watch at all times, praying that you may have strength to escape all these things that will take place, and to stand before the Son of man.
(Luke chapter 21, verses 34 to 36)

K (a)　What event is Jesus talking about?

U (b)　How is Luke's version modifying what Mark writes?

U E (c)　Why do you think Luke is doing this?

K 22　Describe an 'acted parable' from Luke's gospel.

23　Blessed are you poor, for yours is the kingdom of God.
Blessed are you that hunger now, for you shall be satisfied.
Blessed are you that weep now, for you shall laugh.
Blessed are you when men hate you, and when they exclude you and revile you, and cast out your name as evil, on account of the Son of man! Rejoice in that day, and leap for joy, for behold, your

reward is great in heaven; for so their fathers did to the prophets.

(Luke chapter 6, verses 20 to 23)

U
E (a) Explain what Jesus meant by describing such people as blessed.
(b) What kinds of poverty are bad and what kinds of poverty might be considered good?

K 24 Woe to you that are rich, for you have received your consolation.
Woe to you that are full now, for you shall hunger.
Woe to you that laugh now, for you shall mourn and weep.
Woe to you, when all men speak well of you, for so their fathers did to the false prophets.

(Luke chapter 6, verses 24 to 26)

Write in your own words two of Jesus's parables which illustrate any of these woes.

U 25 'The vision of God as presented in the Beatitudes is that of a glorious God.' Comment on this.

U K 26 The disciples could not understand the parable of the Sower, and Jesus had to explain it to them. What do you think Jesus was teaching here? Can you give a modern example of this teaching?

U 27 'Fear not little flock, for it is your Father's good pleasure to give you the kingdom.' What do you think this means?

E 28 Jesus asked, 'What is the kingdom of God like?' and then gave his own answers. How would you describe the kingdom of God? Do you think the idea of God's kingdom governs our lives today?

U 29 How do you interpret the parable of the great banquet?

U K 30 Compare Mark chapter 31, verses 32 to 37, with Luke chapter 21, verses 34 to 36. What do you note about these two passages?

E 31 Why do you think it is perhaps difficult today for anyone to follow the teachings of Jesus?

E 32 'If you love those who love you, what credit is that to you?' What does Jesus mean by this statement? In your own experience, have you found it difficult to love your enemies? Why?

6 The way of the cross

A sword shall pierce Mary's heart

That Joseph and Mary were poor people is soon made clear in Luke's gospel. The Jewish law ordered that a woman who gave birth to a child should make a sacrifice of a lamb in the Jerusalem Temple. If she and her husband could not afford a lamb, a pair of turtledoves or two young pigeons would do instead. According to Luke, Mary could afford only the turtledoves. (chapter 2, verse 24)

This was the humble woman to whom God gave the gift of bearing his special son. But it was a gift which involved suffering as well as happiness.

'A sword will pierce through your own soul.' These were the words which a devout old man named Simeon said in the Jerusalem Temple to Jesus's mother when she brought there her newly born baby to make the sacrifice of turtledoves. Already Luke is telling us that Jesus's life (and so also that of his mother) will be one of suffering. (chapter 2, verse 35)

False ways rejected by Jesus

After Jesus had been baptised by John the Baptist he spent forty days in the wilderness, tempted by the enemy of all men and women, 'the devil', who represents all those attractive but misleading ways we must reject. During those forty days, Luke tells us that Jesus ate nothing. The devil first suggested that if Jesus was the Son of God, he should turn the little pieces of limestone in the desert into bread, to appease his own hunger.

Here the devil is urging Jesus to offer not just to himself but also to other people material goods, as a kind of bribe for following him. Jesus turns on the devil with a sentence from the Jewish Bible: 'It is written, "Man shall not live by bread alone." ' (Deuteronomy chapter 8, verse 3)

Next the devil, Luke states, 'showed him all the kingdoms of the world in a moment of time', and said, 'To you I will give all this authority and their glory.' He added one condition: 'If you will worship me, all will be yours.'

Jesus's reply this time combined two sayings from the Jewish Bible. 'It is written, "You shall worship the Lord your God, and him only shall you serve." ' (Deuteronomy chapter 6, verse 13, and chapter 10, verse 20)

Finally the devil took Jesus to what Luke describes as 'the pinnacle of the Temple'. In fact the Temple in Jesus's day was topped with several exquisite gilded pinnacles. The highest rose some 150 metres above the Kedron valley. From one of these pinnacles, perhaps the highest, the devil argued, Jesus should throw himself down. Since Jesus had used the Bible to disagree with the devil, the devil himself now quoted Scripture himself: 'God will give his angels charge of you, to guard you; on his hands they will bear you up, lest you strike your foot against a stone.' (Psalm 91, verses 11f)

Already we have seen that Jesus refused to use his remarkable God-given powers to persuade people to follow him simply because he could work miracles. Here, at the beginning of his ministry, he makes it clear to the devil that this method is absolutely rejected. Only by following Jesus because you believe his message is true will anyone become a true disciple. Jesus then quotes the Bible again: 'It is said, "You shall not tempt the Lord your God." ' (Deuteronomy chapter 6, verse 16)

So, we learn from Luke, the devil left Jesus, though he remained waiting in the wings till he could return. The devil made his return when Jesus's disciple Judas Iscariot betrayed his master. Here again, then, we find Jesus's suffering and death foreshadowed at the beginning of Luke's gospel. (chapter 4, verses 1 to 13)

Jesus in conflict

Soon Jesus was increasingly at odds with his enemies. Luke narrates a series of stories illustrating the conflict between them. Sometimes when Jesus healed the sick, he was given no credit for it, especially when he did this on the sabbath day of rest, when no one was supposed to work.

Lord of the sabbath

He obviously had taught his followers to look to the *spirit* of the laws of God, not to obey these laws blindly. So one day, Luke tells us:

> On a sabbath, while he was going through the grainfields, his disciples plucked and ate some heads of grain, rubbing them in their hands. But some of the Pharisees said, 'Why are you doing what is not lawful to do on the sabbath?' Jesus reminded them that when King David and his followers were extremely hungry, they

ate holy bread from the Temple. He added, 'The Son of man is lord of the sabbath.'

(chapter 6, verses 1 to 5)

Luke follows this story by telling us that on another sabbath Jesus healed a man's withered right hand. He knew that the scribes and the Pharisees were watching him to see if he would do this. In their view he was breaking God's law. Jesus responded by asking them, 'Is it lawful on the sabbath to do good or to do harm, to save life or to destroy it?'

What are laws for?

His question forced them (and forces us) to ask what laws are for. The question is still important. Here is a report from the *Daily Mail* of 29 November 1988:

Law traps fireman in fast lane

A fireman was ordered to drive the wrong way up the A1 in a life-or-death call – and ended up in court.

Police charged Trevor Kiely, 30, with reckless driving.

But yesterday a judge told him: 'You showed no irresponsibility in any way' and cleared him after the prosecution offered no evidence.

Lincoln Crown Court heard how Mr Kiely became caught in a traffic jam going north near Grantham, Lincolnshire, as he rushed to save people trapped in a blazing car. His control room ordered him to drive down the south-bound fast lane instead.

The part-time fireman from Corby Glen, Lincolnshire, was charged after arriving at the scene to find colleagues had dealt with the emergency.

(*Daily Mail*, 29 November 1988)

This fireman broke the law to do good, not evil. Is it lawful to break the law for such a good purpose, was the essence of Jesus's question. But Jesus's enemies failed to see his point. Luke says that 'they were filled with fury and discussed with one another what they might do to Jesus'. (chapter 6, verses 6 to 11)

Two more healings bring both love and hatred for Jesus

Twice more Luke (and Luke alone of the gospel writers) recalls Jesus healing sick people and being attacked for doing so.

A sick woman in a synagogue

In a synagogue one sabbath day Jesus healed a woman who had been ill for eighteen years. She joyfully gave thanks to God, but the ruler of the synagogue, Luke tells us, was 'indignant'. He complained that, 'There are six days on which work ought to be done; come on those days and be healed, and not on the sabbath day.'

Jesus replied, 'You hypocrites! Does not each of you on the sabbath untie his ox or his ass from the manger, and lead it away to water it?' On this occasion we learn that his adversaries were put to shame and all the people rejoiced. (chapter 13, verses 10 to 17)

A man with dropsy

Then, he was eating with a Pharisee and healed a man suffering dropsy (an accumulation of fluid in the body). Again he asked the lawyers and the Pharisees if it was lawful or not to heal on the sabbath day. Again he drew their attention to their own contradictory and hypocritical behaviour. 'Which of you, having a son or an ox that has fallen into a well, will not immediately pull him out on a sabbath day?' This time not one of them could say a word in reply. (chapter 14, verses 1 to 6)

An attempt to kill Jesus at Nazareth

This pattern of conflict began at the very start of Jesus's ministry, when he preached in the synagogue at Nazareth, where he had been brought up. We have already seen how here Jesus announced to the startled worshippers that his own coming had fulfilled Isaiah's prophecy about the good news which God's messenger would one day bring. (See above, pages 5–6.)

At first, we learn, people were puzzled. Jesus's words were gracious; but, they asked, wasn't he simply the son of Joseph, whom they all knew?

Knowing that his own neighbours had these doubts about him, Jesus began to hint that the good news he was offering, if rejected by his fellow-Jews, could readily be given instead to the Gentiles. He gave two examples from the scriptures to back up what he said.

First, he told how the prophet Elijah never once helped an Israelite widow but only a heathen widow who lived in Zarephath in the land of Sidon; and secondly, he said, although there were many Israelite lepers at the time of the prophet Elisha, Elisha healed only one leper, and he was a Syrian. 'Truly, I say to you, no prophet is acceptable in his own country,' Jesus concluded.

His hearers were enraged. Luke says that 'they rose up and cast him forth out of the city, and led him to the brow of the hill whereon their city was built, that they might throw him down headlong. But he passing through the midst of them went his way.' (chapter 4, verses 22 to 30)

He went his way

The earliest Christians used to call their pattern of life 'the way'. For Jesus and for many of them it was the way of crucifixion and death.

Christians distribute palms to remember that when Jesus rode into Jerusalem some people put palm leaves and branches along his way.

Jesus's way as Luke describes it led him through Galilee and Samaria to Jerusalem, where he was to be put to death. Luke records that he said, 'I must go on my way today and tomorrow and the day following; for it cannot be that a prophet should perish away from Jerusalem.' (chapter 13, verse 33)

Riding into Jerusalem

Jesus as we see him in Luke's gospel becomes more and more determined to reach Jerusalem where he is to be crucified. His fearful disciples seem to be holding back but, Luke writes, 'he went on ahead, going up to Jerusalem'.

Reaching the Mount of Olives outside the city, he sent two of his disciples into a nearby village to bring him a colt that nobody had yet ridden. The owners of the colt, seeing the disciples untying it, asked what they were doing. The two disciples answered, as Jesus had instructed them, 'The Lord has need of it.'

When Jesus rode into Jerusalem on the colt, his followers spread their clothing on the road in front of him, crying out, 'Blessed is the King who comes in the name of the Lord! Peace in heaven and glory in the highest!'

Luke is quoting Psalm 118, verse 26 here, but he adds the word 'King' which is not found in that psalm. He wishes to show that Jesus's followers supposed he was coming to Jerusalem to fulfil another important Bible prophecy. In the book of the prophet Zechariah (chapter 9, verses 9f), the Jews were promised that one day just such a king would ride into Jerusalem — not on a war horse but on a colt, and bringing not war but peace:

> Rejoice greatly, O daughter of Zion!
>   Shout aloud, O daughter of Jerusalem!
> Lo, your king comes to you;
>   triumphant and victorious is he,
> humble and riding on an ass,
>   on a colt, the foal of an ass . . .
>   and he shall command peace to the nations.

Yet even the King bringing peace was hated by some onlookers. Some of the Pharisees in the crowd told Jesus to rebuke his disciples for welcoming him in this rapturous way. Jesus replied, 'I tell you, if these were silent, the very stones would cry out.' (chapter 19, verses 28 to 40)

Jerusalem and its Temple

By the time he arrived for the last time at his beloved Jerusalem, Jesus had already described the city as 'forsaken'. Jerusalem had rejected his love. He cried out, as Luke records, 'O Jerusalem, Jerusalem, killing the prophets and stoning those who are sent to you! How often would I have gathered your children together as a hen gathers her brood under her wings, and you would not!' (chapter 13, verse 34)

Later, when people were describing the beauty of the Jerusalem Temple, 'how it was adorned with noble stones and offerings', Jesus said, 'As for these things which you see, the days will come when there shall not be left one stone upon another that will not be thrown down.' (chapter 21, verses 5f). By the time Luke wrote his gospel, he probably knew that Jesus's prediction had come about, for in AD 70 the armies of Rome had attacked Jerusalem and destroyed its Temple. Luke makes Jesus specifically foretell this destruction of the city. 'Jerusalem', Jesus prophesies, 'will be trodden down by the Gentiles.' (chapter 21, verse 24)

Luke tells us that Jesus wept over Jerusalem. 'Your enemies will cast up a bank about you, and hem you in on every side, and dash you to the ground, you and your children within you, and they will not leave one stone upon another in you.' (chapter 19, verses 43f.) Many scholars think that Luke has changed Jesus's words here because he knew that the Romans had built a wall or 'bank' around the city when they attacked it. Luke makes Jesus's words fit in with what happened later.

Jesus cleanses the Temple

Immediately after this we learn from Luke that Jesus entered the Temple and began to drive out those who sold doves there, saying to them, 'It is written, "My house shall be a house of prayer; but you have made it a den of thieves." '

His mother, as we have already seen, made a sacrifice of doves in the Jerusalem Temple when Jesus was born. Merchants sold these doves in the Temple. They also changed money for foreigners who wanted to pay the annual Temple tax of half a shekel (which amounted to almost two days' pay for the average working man of that time).

Although Jesus said he was returning the Temple to its true function as a house of prayer — as it was described by the prophet Isaiah (chapter 56, verse 7) — his action brought closer his capture, trial and death. From this moment he began to teach in the Temple every day. All the people, we are told, 'hung on his words'. But Luke adds that, 'The chief priests and the scribes and the principal men of the people sought to destroy him.' (chapter 19, verses 45 to 47)

Judas agrees to betray Jesus

The devil has been absent from Luke's story since Jesus's temptation in the wilderness. Now we are told he 'entered into' one of Jesus's twelve disciples, a man named Judas Iscariot. The chief priests and other leaders offered him money if he would betray Jesus to them. Even though Jesus was acclaimed by great crowds, as we have already seen when he secretly arranged the loan of the colt, he was now taking great care not to let his movements be known to his enemies.

Everything he did was kept secret. This was the time of the most important Jewish festival of the year, the feast of the Passover, when families and groups of friends would come together in Jerusalem for a special meal to remember how Moses long ago had led their ancestors to freedom from the rule of the Egyptians. Jesus and his disciples planned to celebrate such a meal. Once more he kept their arrangements a close secret. He sent his disciples Peter and John into Jerusalem. There, as Jesus had told them, they met a man carrying a jar of water who took them to a furnished upper room. In that room they arranged everything for the feast of the Passover. It was to be Jesus's last supper with them before his death.

The Last Supper

Today Christians see this Last Supper as the inspiration for their Holy Communion or Eucharist, for Jesus told his followers that they should

A Jewish nomad family celebrating their first Passover since arriving in Palestine.

repeat the solemn meal 'in remembrance of me'. The feast of the Passover involved drinking cups of wine and eating bread which had no leaven (for making dough rise) in it. Just before giving this command Jesus had broken a piece of this bread, saying, 'This is my body, which is given for you.' Clearly Jesus saw that his death on the cross was certain. His body would be broken, just as he now broke the bread.

His blood too would pour out of his veins as he died, nailed to a cross of wood. So when he filled a cup of wine and offered it to them, he said, 'This cup which is poured out for you is the new covenant in my blood.'

The word 'covenant' refers to an agreement between God and human beings which the Jews loved to read about in the book of Exodus (chapter 24, verses 1 to 8). There, they learned, Moses on their behalf had agreed that they should keep all God's commands. In return God would specially care for them. To seal this agreement, Moses had thrown ox blood on the altar of God and over all the people.

Remembering this, Jesus was making a new, special relationship, between himself and his twelve disciples, a relationship which his followers today still remember when they obey his command to repeat this act of worship with bread and wine. It was to be sealed not in ox blood but in his own blood.

Serving, obeying and betraying

Since this was a moment of extreme danger, Jesus also spoke of what it meant to follow him. First he told them of the demands laid on a disciple. Whereas most kings pretended that they ruled out of love for their underlings, Jesus saw through this pretence. He told his disciples not to imitate this hypocrisy:

> Rather let the greatest among you become as the youngest; and the leader as one who serves. For which is the greater, one who sits at table or one who serves? Is it not the one who sits at table? But I am among you as one who serves.

(chapter 22, verses 26f)

Here Jesus is turning completely upside-down the way the world gives honour to rulers rather than servants.

Next he predicted that even his loyal disciple Simon Peter would fail him. Sensing the danger of that moment, Peter said to him, 'Lord, I am ready to go with you to prison and to death.' Jesus answered, 'I tell you Peter, the cock will not crow this day, until you three times deny that you know me.' This proved to be the terrible truth. While Jesus was on trial, Peter was warming himself by a fire in the courtyard of the high priest's house when a maid three times accused him of being one of the disciples. Three times Peter denied it. The third time, while he was still speaking, a cock crowed. Jesus turned round and looked at Peter, says Luke; and Peter went out and wept bitterly.

Thirdly, Jesus said that one of his disciples, Judas, was ready to betray him. 'Behold the hand of him who betrays me is with me on the table,' he said. Although Jesus now believed that it was his destiny to follow the way of the cross, he did not believe that this forgave Judas and the ones who were to be responsible for his death. 'The Son of man goes as it has been determined,' he said, adding, 'but woe to that man by whom he is betrayed.' (chapter 22, verses 14 to 34 and verses 54 to 62)

Then he went to the Mount of Olives, and knelt down, begging God to spare him the coming torment. Even so, Jesus added, 'nevertheless, not my will, but thine be done.' Is it surprising that even Jesus was afraid to be tortured to death? 'If you take away due fear,' declared John Donne, the seventeenth-century poet and Christian, 'you take away true love.'

Jesus came down from the Mount of Olives and found his disciples asleep. As soon as he woke them, a crowd appeared; among them Judas. Judas's secret sign to identify Jesus was to kiss him. 'Judas,' said Jesus, 'would you betray the Son of man with a kiss?' He stopped his other disciples from defending him with swords, and was arrested. (chapter 22, verses 39 to 53)

The trials of Jesus

Jesus was tried three times. The first trial took place before the Jewish Council, the other two before Pontius Pilate and before Herod Antipas.

Both the Council and Herod allowed their innocent prisoner to be mistreated. When he was in the care of the Council, the men holding him mocked and beat him. They put a blindfold over his eyes and then struck him again, mockingly asking him to state who had hit him. Herod and his soldiers also treated Jesus with contempt, mocking him by dressing him as a king in gorgeous clothing before sending him back to Pontius Pilate, who — as the representative of Roman power — was the only man able to sentence Jesus to death.

The charges

Before the Jewish Council

The chief priests and the Jewish Council were angry mainly because Jesus claimed to be the Christ. This, they believed, insulted God. Luke tells us that when they explicitly asked him if he thought he was the Christ, Jesus refused to give a direct answer, saying instead, 'If I tell you, you will not believe.' He continued with the words, 'But from now on the Son of man shall be seated at the right hand of the power of God.'

This claim infuriated them. They all asked, 'Are you the Son of God, then.' Again Jesus did not answer directly. His reply was, 'You say that I am.' This was enough for the Council. 'What further testimony do we need?' they cried. 'We have heard it ourselves from his own lips.' (chapter 22, verses 63 to 71)

Before Herod Antipas

Herod seems to have had no interest in these religious questions. He had obviously heard about Jesus's miracles. For a long time, Luke says, he had wanted to see Jesus, 'hoping to see some sign done by him'. Jesus simply refused to speak to him, even though the chief priests and the scribes were standing by, viciously attacking him. (chapter 23, verses 6 to 12)

Before Pontius Pilate

As the Roman ruler, Pilate was interested in Jesus's political views. Was he a revolutionary or not? Jesus's enemies told Pilate that he had tried to persuade people not to pay their taxes to Caesar. In addition they claimed that Jesus had set himself up as king, in opposition to Caesar. Jesus, they were claiming, was a political rebel.

Pilate found these charges untrue. Like Herod, he decided that Jesus was innocent, even though he was willing to chastise him before releasing him. Unfortunately, Pilate was also weak. He asked the chief

Must we always obey the law? A Dominican nun is arrested for breaking into a US airforce base in 1989 as a demonstration against nuclear weapons.

priests and scribes if they wanted Jesus set free. But they demanded the release of a rebel and a murderer named Barabbas instead. As for Jesus, they cried, 'Crucify, crucify him!' Pilate gave way. (chapter 23, verses 1 to 5 and 13 to 24)

Jesus is crucified

Even though Pilate accepted that Jesus was not a revolutionary who was setting himself up as king against Caesar, Luke tells us that over his cross were the words, 'This is the King of the Jews.' Was this written to mock Jesus? The Roman soldiers around the cross certainly laughed at him, with the words, 'If you are the King of the Jews, save yourself.'

Others mocked him for claiming to be the Christ. 'He saved others,' they said; 'let him save himself, if he is the Christ of God, the Chosen One!' Two criminals were also crucified, one on either side of Jesus. When one of them mocked Jesus, too, with the words, 'Are you not the Christ? Save yourself and us!', he was rebuked by his fellow, who said that the two of them were being justly punished, but Jesus was innocent. Turning to Jesus, this criminal begged, 'Remember me when you come into your kingdom.'

Jesus forgives while hanging on the cross

Here Luke's concern to show Jesus's love for the outcast once again appears. Jesus replied to the criminal, 'Truly, I say to you, today you will be with me in Paradise.' Jesus is also portrayed as showing mercy even on those who crucified him. Luke tells us that on the cross he cried, 'Father, forgive them; they know not what they do.' As St Augustine wrote, 'The cross upon which was fixed the body of the dying Jesus was also the chair in which the Master sat as a teacher.' As he was dying, he taught us to forgive our enemies.

Dead and buried

When he was arrested, Jesus had said to his enemies, 'This is your hour; this is the reign of darkness.' Darkness stands here for utter evil, and Luke now reminds us of this when Jesus dies on the cross. For three hours, he tells us, there was darkness over the whole land. Jesus then cried out, 'Father, into thy hands I commend my spirit,' and died. So his last words, according to Luke, were from Psalm 31, the words used by Jewish children as they lay down at night to sleep.

He had no grave of his own. A good man, a member of the Jewish Council named Joseph of Arimathea who had not agreed with the condemnation of Jesus, asked Pontius Pilate for Jesus's body, wrapped it in a linen shroud and placed it in a tomb carved out of a rock. A stone was rolled up against the mouth of this tomb. Luke records this because he wants us to be absolutely certain that Jesus was dead and buried.

Some of the women who followed Jesus planned to anoint the body with spices, but they put off this plan because it was the sabbath day when they did not work. (chapter 23, verses 44 to 56)

Deeper meanings

As he tells his story, Luke is always hinting at deeper meanings. For example, when Jesus died Luke says that the Temple veil was torn in two. Only the high priest had been allowed beyond that veil. Luke is suggesting that Jesus has, by his death, somehow opened up the innermost secrets of God to everyone.

A second hint at a deeper meaning to the crucifixion is put in by Luke just as some of Jesus's disciples are about to resist his arrest, by using swords against the crowd. Jesus tells them that he must now suffer, in order that his life will fulfil a saying of the prophet Isaiah, 'He was reckoned with the transgressors.' (Luke chapter 22, verse 37, and Isaiah chapter 53, verse 12)

This reference is to a famous passage in which Isaiah is describing God's servant, a man who will suffer on behalf of others. The same verse states that this suffering servant 'bore the sin of many'. Isaiah declares that 'he was wounded for our transgressions, he was bruised for our iniquities; upon him was the chastisement that made us whole, and with his stripes we are healed'. (chapter 53, verse 5)

This notion of a sinless person bearing the sins of others is difficult to understand. Yet here is a modern example, though not one which approaches Jesus's supreme sacrifice, in a report from the *Daily Telegraph* of 29 August 1986:

Mother bought drugs to wean son off habit

by Paul Stokes

A mother told yesterday how she risked prison to buy hard drugs from a pusher in order to wean her son off his addiction to cocaine.

Mrs Jean Bird and her husband Roger, both 47, spent hundreds of pounds of their own cash and worked 80 hours a week to finance their 19-year-old son Paul's £100-a-day habit.

They agreed to buy the drugs for him to control his intake, and reduce his dependence, after he had begged them for help. They supplied him with less and less each day.

'I hated it,' said Mrs Bird a garage supervisor, of Whitmead Gardens, Hartcliffe, Bristol. 'It was degrading, but there was no other way to get him off them. It was lovely to watch him change back to normal and get healthier.'

Luke shows us Jesus willingly accepting his fate: 'Jesus suffers in his passion the torments which men inflict on him,' wrote the French philosopher Blaise Pascal; 'but in his agony he also suffers the torments which he inflicts on himself.'

Fulfilling the promises of the prophets

Why did Jesus accept such torments? Luke paints the picture of a man whose life was patterned on God's own will, expressed long before his time, through the words of the Old Testament prophets. Luke wants to show that nothing that happened to Jesus happened by chance. Everything was done in obedience to God's plan to save sinful men and women.

The empty tomb

Early on Sunday morning several women, including Mary Magdalene, Joanna, and Mary the mother of James, came to embalm Jesus's body. To their amazement they found that the stone sealing the tomb had been rolled away. Jesus's body was no longer there. Instead two men appeared, wearing dazzling clothing. The frightened women bowed before them, as the men asked them, 'Why do you seek the living among the dead?'

They reminded the women that Jesus had foretold that three days after his death, he would rise again. The women, remembering this, returned to Jesus's disciples — now only eleven because Judas had deserted them — to give them the good news, but the disciples refused to believe it. (chapter 24, verses 1 to 11)

The road to Emmaus

Two of the disciples then set off for a village called Emmaus, which lay about seven miles from Jerusalem. On the way Jesus joined them, though (Luke says) 'their eyes were kept from recognising him'.

These two disciples poured out to this apparent stranger all that they had hoped of Jesus. They told him of the women's strange report about the empty tomb. Jesus then accused them of being too foolish and slow-witted to understand that everything that had happened to him had been in accordance with God's plan as revealed through his prophets. 'It was necessary,' he explained, 'that the Christ should suffer these things and enter into his glory.' And he set about showing how all this could have been seen by anyone who truly understood the scriptures.

So they reached Emmaus. Jesus was about to go further, but the two disciples persuaded him to take a meal with them. Only as he broke the bread did they recognise him. Then he vanished. (chapter 24, verses 13 to 31)

Jesus has appeared to Simon

Overwhelmed with this vision, the two disciples instantly returned to Jerusalem to tell their fellows what had happened. There they were told that Jesus had also appeared to Simon Peter.

The two disciples also stressed that it was in the 'breaking of bread' (the earliest Christian name for the Eucharist, Holy Communion or Mass) that he was known to them. Here Luke seems to be confirming that in obeying Jesus's command to repeat the Last Supper his followers would again and again meet him for the rest of time. (chapter 24, verses 32 to 35)

A real person

Obviously someone who can appear and disappear is not a normal man. Were these visions of Jesus false and unreal? Luke was aware that people would accuse the disciples of seeing not Jesus himself but what he calls 'a spirit'. But, he tells us, as the disciples discussed all that had happened, again Jesus stood among them.

Frightened, at first they believed that what they saw was a spirit. To convince them that he was really alive again, Jesus asked them to feel him. He was, he said, 'flesh and bones'. To prove it he asked for something to eat, and they gave him a piece of broiled fish.

Once again he explained that all that had happened to him could have been read in the prophecies of the Bible. The prophet Hosea, for example (in chapter 6, verse 2) had declared that after three days God would raise his faithful servant from death. Isaiah had written about how God's true servant must suffer. All this had happened to Jesus. (chapter 24, verses 36 to 46)

The mission of the disciples

At the very beginning of Jesus's ministry his cousin John the Baptist had prepared the way for him by urging sinners to repent and be forgiven by God. Jesus had already shown that he possessed God's authority to forgive sins (see pages 34–36).

Now he ordered his disciples to begin in Jerusalem and then preach the same repentance and forgiveness to the whole world. In Jerusalem, where Luke's story began, God, Jesus promised, would 'clothe' the disciples 'with power from on high', so that they would be strong enough to carry out this task. So Luke prepares his readers for his second book, the Acts of the Apostles, where he tells of the disciples' heroic exploits, all carried out in the power of God's spirit. (chapter 24, verses 47 to 49)

Jesus's final journey

Luke ends his gospel with the words:

> Then he led them out as far as Bethany, and lifting his hands he blessed them. While he blessed them, he parted from them, and was carried up into heaven. And they returned to Jerusalem with great joy, and were continually in the temple blessing God.
>
> (chapter 24, verses 50 to 52)

Joy

Joy is a word mentioned more in Luke's gospel than in any other of the four. Friends of Jesus *rejoice* when his enemies are put to shame. Jesus even talks about *joy in heaven*. 'I bring you good news of *a great joy* which will come to all the people,' the angel had sung to the shepherds, when announcing the birth of Jesus (chapter 2, verse 10). Told she was to bear the baby Jesus, Mary sang:

> My soul magnifies the Lord,
> and my spirit *rejoices* in God my Saviour.
>
> (chapter 1, verses 46f)

The good news of Jesus brings joy to earth. (See also pages 22–24, 50.)

Heaven

The statement that Jesus was taken up into heaven is not found in some of our oldest texts of Luke's gospel. Perhaps the people who copied out his gospel for us felt uncertain where 'heaven' is.

Is heaven somewhere in the sky? More likely it is a completely different universe from ours. Scientists today have no problem about believing in new universes, parallel to ours. (If this subject interests you, you can read about it in John D Barrow's book *The World Within the World*, Clarendon Press, 1988.)

Worship

Luke's gospel also ends on a note of worship. Jesus is in glory, and his status as Son of God is now utterly secure. 'Henceforth,' as Archbishop Michael Ramsey put it, 'the worship of Jesus and the praise of God are inseparably blended.' (A M Ramsey, *The Resurrection of Christ*, revised edition, Fontana Books, 1961, p. 81)

Assignments

E 1 'Luke's gospel from the very start presents us with a tragedy.' If you believe this is true, illustrate the statement by describing episodes from Luke's gospel.

K U 2 What are 'conflict stories'? Give two examples from Luke's gospel.

K E 3 'Is it lawful on the sabbath to do good or to do harm, to save life or to destroy it?' Describe the occasion on which Jesus asked this question. What was the response of his hearers? How would you respond to the question?

4 Luke tells us that Jesus sent the following message to King Herod, 'Behold I cast out demons and perform cures today and tomorrow, and the third day I must finish my course.'

U   (a) What do you think Jesus means by the words, 'the third day I must finish my course'.

K   (b) Describe in your own words:
       (1) Jesus casting out a demon.
       (2) Jesus performing a cure.

K 5 'I tell you, if these were silent, the very stones would cry out.' Give an account of the occasion when Jesus said this.

K 6 Describe in your own words the trials of Jesus before (a) the Jewish Council; (b) Herod Antipas; and (c) Pontius Pilate.

U 7 Jesus, just before he was arrested and crucified, quoted to his disciples the words of the prophet Isaiah: 'He was reckoned with the transgressors.' What did he mean by this?

U K 8 In the words of the French Christian, Blaise Pascal, 'Jesus suffers in his passion the torments which men inflict on him, but in his agony he also suffers the torments which he inflicts on himself.' In what ways does Luke's gospel show Jesus inflicting torments on himself?

U 9 St Augustine wrote, 'The cross upon which was fixed the body of the dying Jesus was also the chair in which the Master sat as a teacher.' What did Jesus teach on the cross?

118

K 10 'Jesus spent forty days and forty nights in the wilderness and was tempted by the devil.' What were the suggestions made by the devil, and how did Jesus answer them?

K 11 Often Jesus was at odds with his enemies. Give three examples of these occasions.

E 12 Read the extract from the *Daily Mail* on page 104 and in groups discuss whether or not it is lawful to break the law for good purposes.

K 13 Give two accounts of times when Jesus healed sick people and was attacked for doing so.

K U 14 Throughout Luke's gospel follow the pattern of conflict in Jesus's adult life.

K 15 The earliest Christians used to call their pattern of life 'the Way'. Which 'way' did Jesus follow?

U E 16 Jesus described the city of Jerusalem as 'forsaken'. Give his reasons for this.

K U 17 Give a detailed account of the Last Supper. Why is this Last Supper still important for Christians today? What does the word 'covenant' mean?

K 18 Jesus told his disciples what it would mean to follow him. What did he say?

K 19 Prepare in groups a play based on the trials of Jesus — before the Jewish Council, Pontius Pilate and Herod Antipas.

K E 20 Describe in your own words the crucifixion of Jesus. What in your view does it mean for us today?

K 21 Pretend that you are Mary Magdalene. Describe in detail your visit to Jesus's tomb on the Sunday morning after his crucifixion.

K 22 Describe what happened on the road to Emmaus. Read very carefully what was said by Jesus and by the disciples. What was the mood of the disciples, and what was that of Jesus? When did the disciples recognise Jesus?

K U 23 Someone who can appear and disappear is not a normal human being. How, according to Luke, did Jesus after his resurrection convince his followers that he was really alive? Why is this important for Christians today?

K 24 What did the risen Jesus command his disciples to do?

K 25 What are the differences between Mark's account and Luke's account of the events after Jesus's death and burial?

General questions

K U 1   What makes Luke's gospel different from the other gospels?

K U 2   What does Jesus teach about prayer, according to Luke's gospel? Discuss prayer with six people you know, find out their views and report back to your group.

K 3   'Luke's gospel is a joyful one.' Can you support this statement with examples from the gospel?

U 4   Who was Jesus? Use Luke's gospel in giving your answer.

E 5   Luke wrote much about sinners and the poor. What did he say about them? Is what he wrote useful today?

E 6   Luke states very clearly the dangers of possessing much wealth. Look at some wealthy people who are, or have been, well known (e.g. Christina Onassis). Has wealth made them happy?

E 7   The problems of the poor are always being brought to our attention. Read your newspapers and identify some groups of poor people. By relating what you have found to Luke's gospel, how would you respond to their problems?

E 8   What is the World Council of Churches? (To find out, you might have to visit your local library.) How does this organisation fit in with Luke's gospel? (Read Luke chapter 7, verses 36 to 50.)

E 9   If you could run your own society, what would it be like? How would it fit in with the views of Jesus as reported by Luke?

E 10   Today the Anglican Church is split over the question whether women can be ordained priests. Visit your public library and find from the *Church Times* the arguments for and against the ordination of women. Give your views, taking into consideration the opinion of the Roman Catholic Church.

U E 11   Many people today are prejudiced against others. Cut out newspaper articles, mount them on cardboard, and then write down what you think. What makes people prejudiced against others?

U 12 'Luke's gospel is a social gospel.' What does this mean? What aspects of present-day political life does Luke's gospel illuminate?

E 13 Do you think that the Christian churches should interfere in or preach about politics?

U 14 Read the following newspaper article, and then write about how Cardinal Basil Hume's words relate to Luke's gospel.

E U 15 Look up the different meanings of LOVE as found in Luke's gospel. Find examples of these kinds of love in poetry, novels, people's lives, newspaper reports. Comment on them either from a Christian or from a non-Christian viewpoint.

E U 16 What elements in the teaching of Jesus as set out by Luke fit in with our lives today? Take relevant passages from his gospel and relate them to current events and our own daily lives.

U E 17 Write down all you can discover in Luke's gospel about Jesus's family. From this information, try to describe what Luke would regard as a Christian family. Say in what ways twentieth-century families live up to his ideal and in what ways they fall down.

U 18 How does Luke's gospel reveal the author's interests and his intentions in writing it?

U 19 Why did Luke write his gospel?

E 20 'Luke depicts Jesus as both the friend and the saviour of men and women.' Comment on this statement.

These are all members of one family — the Sheltons of Islington have several adopted children.

122

K 21 Without repentance and faith the full meaning of the parables would be hidden. With reference to Luke's gospel, show what this statement means.

U E 22 Why did Jesus die? Does his death have any relevance to our lives today?

K U 23 What are the message and the challenge of the parables for twentieth-century families?

7 A detailed breakdown of Luke's gospel

Introduction

chapter 1, verses 1 to 4.

The beginning of the age of the Messiah

An angel appears to Zechariah in the Jerusalem Temple: chapter 1, verses 5 to 25.
An angel appears to the Virgin Mary: chapter 1, verses 26 to 38.
Mary sings of her own joy and about her unborn son: chapter 1, verses 39 to 56.
Zechariah's wife gives birth to John the Baptist: chapter 1, verses 57 to 66.
Zechariah sings of his son's future: chapter 1, verses 67 to 80.
Jesus is born in a stable: chapter 2, verses 1 to 7.
The shepherds worship him: chapter 2, verses 8 to 20.
In the Jerusalem Temple a devout Jew sings of Jesus's future: chapter 2, verses 21 to 40.

Jesus's ministry begins

At the age of twelve Jesus visits Jerusalem: chapter 2, verses 41 to 52.
The preaching of John the Baptist: chapter 3, verses 1 to 20.
Jesus is baptised by John: chapter 3, verses 21f.
Luke lists Jesus's ancestors: chapter 3, verses 23 to 38.
Jesus is tempted by the devil: chapter 4, verses 1 to 13.
He preaches in the synagogue at Nazareth: chapter 4, verses 14 to 30.

The Messiah in action

Healing the sick of Capernaum: chapter 4, verses 31 to 44.
A huge catch of fish: chapter 5, verses 1 to 11.

A leper is healed: chapter 5, verses 12 to 16.
Jesus heals and forgives the sins of a paralysed man: chapter 5, verses 17 to 26.
Jesus calls a tax collector named Levi to follow him: chapter 5, verses 27f.
Jesus at Levi's great feast: chapter 5, verses 29 to 39.
At work even on the sabbath day: chapter 6, verses 1 to 11.
Jesus chooses his twelve apostles: chapter 6, verses 12 to 16.

The teachings of Jesus

The Beatitudes: chapter 6, verses 17 to 31.
True love: chapter 6, verses 32 to 38.
Parables of good and evil: chapter 6, verses 39 to 49.

Miracles and teaching

Jesus heals a Roman centurion's slave: chapter 7, verses 1 to 10.
He raises a widow's son from death: chapter 7, verses 11 to 17.
He teaches about John the Baptist: chapter 7, verses 18 to 35.
The Pharisee and the sinful woman: chapter 7, verses 36 to 50.
Jesus, the apostles and some women preach the good news: chapter 8, verses 1 to 3.
The parable of the sower: chapter 8, verses 4 to 15.
The parable of the lamp: chapter 8, verses 16 to 18.
The true family of Jesus: chapter 8, verses 19 to 21.
Jesus calms a storm: chapter 8, verses 22 to 25.
He heals a man tormented with demons: chapter 8, verses 26 to 39.
He heals a woman's haemhorrhage and raises a dead girl: chapter 8, verses 40 to 56.
The disciples are given authority to heal and preach: chapter 9, verses 1 to 6.

Who is Jesus?

Herod is puzzled about Jesus: chapter 9, verses 7 to 9.
Jesus cures more sick people: chapter 9, verses 10f.
He feeds five thousand people: chapter 9, verses 12 to 17.
Peter declares that he believes Jesus is 'the Christ of God': chapter 9, verses 18 to 22.
What it means to follow Jesus: chapter 9, verses 23 to 27.
The transfiguration of Jesus: chapter 9, verses 28 to 36.
He heals an epileptic boy: chapter 9, verses 37 to 45.

Following or rejecting Jesus

The greatest in the kingdom of God: chapter 9, verses 46 to 50.
Jesus is rejected in Samaria: chapter 9, verses 51 to 56.
Jesus the homeless one: chapter 9, verses 57 to 62.
The disciples too are sometimes welcomed and sometimes rejected: chapter 10, verses 1 to 20.
Who are the blessed ones? chapter 10, verses 21 to 24.
The parable of the good Samaritan: chapter 10, verses 25 to 37.
Martha and Mary receive Jesus in their home: chapter 10, verses 38 to 42.

Prayer and power

The Lord's prayer: chapter 11, verses 1 to 4.
Keep on asking — a parable about prayer: chapter 11, verses 5 to 13.
Casting out demons and what it means: chapter 11, verses 14 to 26.
The truly blessed: chapter 11, verses 27f.
The 'sign' of Jonah: chapter 11, verses 29 to 32.
The parable of the lamp: chapter 11, verses 33 to 36.

Father Anthony, a priest in Uganda, has come to pray with this woman who has Aids. Her husband has died of Aids and also five members of his family.

False teachers condemned by Jesus

Condemning Pharisees and dining with one: chapter 11, verses 37 to 44.
Jesus next condemns the lawyers: chapter 11, verses 45 to 52.
His enemies lie in wait: chapter 11, verses 53f.
The Pharisees again condemned: chapter 12, verses 1 to 3.

Suffering triumphantly

Fear not: chapter 12, verses 4 to 12.
True riches: chapter 12, verses 13 to 34.
Be ready for the coming of the master: chapter 12, verses 35 to 48.
Jesus foretells divisions on earth: chapter 12, verses 49 to 53.
Judgment approaches: chapter 12, verses 54 to 59.
Repent or perish: chapter 13, verses 1 to 5.
The parable of the fig tree: chapter 13, verses 6 to 9.
His enemies condemn Jesus for healing on the sabbath day: chapter 13, verses 10 to 17.

The kingdom of God

A grain of mustard seed: chapter 13, verses 18f.
Leaven: chapter 13, verses 20f.
Some will feast, some will be cast out: chapter 13, verses 22 to 30.
Jesus declares that even Jerusalem will be forsaken: chapter 13, verses 31 to 35.
He heals again on the sabbath day: chapter 14, verses 1 to 6.
The parable of the marriage feast: chapter 14, verses 7 to 11.
The feast of the outcasts: chapter 14, verses 12 to 14.
Outcasts invited to the great banquet while others will be refused: chapter 14, verses 15 to 24.
Rejecting all to follow Jesus: chapter 14, verses 25 to 33.
Salt that has become useless: chapter 14, verses 34f.
Three parables about repentant sinners — The lost sheep: chapter 15, verses 1 to 7. The lost coin: chapter 15, verses 8 to 10. The prodigal son: chapter 15, verses 11 to 32.
Riches and the kingdom of God: chapter 16.

Forgiveness and our response

Ourselves and the sins of others: chapter 17, verses 1 to 4.
The faith of a grain of mustard seed: chapter 17, verses 5f.
The parable of the farm labourer: chapter 17, verses 7 to 10.
The grateful Samaritan: chapter 17, verses 11 to 19.

The Son of man and the kingdom of God

When will God's kingdom come on earth?: chapter 17, verses 20f.
What will happen when the Son of man comes: chapter 17, verses 22 to 37.
Faith in persistent prayer: chapter 18, verses 1 to 8.
Who is acceptable to God — a parable about a Pharisee and a tax collector: chapter 18, verses 9 to 14.
Children and the kingdom of God: chapter 18, verses 15 to 17.
Earthly riches and the kingdom of God: chapter 18, verses 18 to 30.

On the way to Jerusalem and death

Jesus talks about his death and resurrection: chapter 18, verses 31 to 34.
Near Jericho he heals a blind man who has faith in him: chapter 18, verses 35 to 43.
At Jericho he stays with a tax collector: chapter 19, verses 1 to 10.
The parable of a nobleman and his ten servants: chapter 19, verses 11 to 27.
Jesus rides into Jerusalem on a donkey: chapter 19, verses 28 to 41.
He predicts the downfall of Jerusalem: chapter 19, verses 41 to 44.

In the Jerusalem Temple among enemies

Jesus cleanses and teaches in the Jerusalem Temple: chapter 19, verse 45 to chapter 20, verse 8.
The story of the wicked tenants: chapter 20, verses 9 to 18.
The scribes and chief priests try to trick Jesus: chapter 20, verses 19 to 26.
The Sadducees ask a trick question about life after death: chapter 20, verses 27 to 44.
Jesus openly condemns the scribes: chapter 20, verses 45 to 47.
He praises a poor widow in the Temple: chapter 21, verses 1 to 4.
The coming fate of the Temple: chapter 21, verses 5 to 7.
He warns the disciples that they too will suffer and then triumph: chapter 21, verses 8 to 19.
Jesus speaks of the destruction of Jerusalem: chapter 21, verses 20 to 24.
The coming of the Son of man: chapter 21, verses 25 to 28.
The parable of the fig tree: chapter 21, verses 29 to 33.
Watch and pray: chapter 21, verses 34 to 36.
A summary of Jesus's daily life at this time: chapter 21, verses 37f.

Jesus in peril

The plot to kill him: chapter 22, verses 1 to 6.
The Last Supper: chapter 22, verses 7 to 38.
On the Mount of Olives: chapter 22, verses 39 to 42.
Judas Iscariot betrays Jesus to his enemies: chapter 22, verses 47 to 53.
Peter's cowardice: chapter 22, verses 54 to 62.
Jesus is beaten and mocked: chapter 22, verses 63 to 65.

Jesus on trial

On trial before the Jerusalem Council: chapter 22, verses 66 to 71.
On trial before Pilate: chapter 23, verses 1 to 5.
On trial before Herod: chapter 23, verses 6 to 12.
The crowd turns against Jesus: chapter 23, verses 13 to 25.

The way of the cross

Jesus on his way to be crucified: chapter 23, verses 26 to 32.
The crucifixion: chapter 23, verses 33 to 38.
The two criminals crucified with Jesus: chapter 23, verses 39 to 43.
Strange events surround Jesus's death: chapter 23, verses 44f.
Jesus dies on the cross: chapter 23, verses 46 to 49.
Jesus is buried: chapter 23, verses 50 to 56.

Jesus rises from death

Women discover his tomb is empty: chapter 24, verses 1 to 10.
Jesus appears to two disciples on the road to Emmaeus: chapter 24, verses 13 to 27.
He eats with them and then vanishes: chapter 24, verses 28 to 31.
They learn that he has also appeared to Peter: chapter 24, verses 32 to 35.
Jesus appears to all his disciples and eats with them: chapter 24, verses 36 to 43.
His last message to his disciples: chapter 24, verses 44 to 49.
He finally leaves them: chapter 24, verses 50 to 53.

Index

Acts of the Apostle 1, 14, 93f., 116
Allegories 86f., 98
Angels 30f. (see also Gabriel)
Apostles 62f,, 71 (see also Disciples,
  Peter and Missionaries)
Ascension 117
Augustine, St., 118

Banquet 40, 90f.
Baptism 23f., 37f.
Barclay, William 46
Beatitudes 95, 100f.
Beelzebul, see Demons
Bethlehem 13, 27f.
Blind 41, 78, 81, 82
Bread, daily 50f., 58, 102

Children 84f., 93
Christ 34f.
Christmas, 32, 38
Church 93
Communion, Holy, 75f., 97, 109f. (see
  also Banquet and Last Supper)
Compassion 79f.
Cross 63f., 71, 102f., 105–13
Crucifixion 19, 105–10, 118f.

Daniel, prophet 25
David, King 22, 34f., 38
Deaf persons 81
Death 9f., 33, 76f., 81, 97, 115, 123
Demons, 34f., 75, 98, 102f. 118f.
Devil, see Demons
Disciples 62, 71, 116f. (see also Apostles
  and Missionaries)

Elijah 24f., 105
Elizabeth 26f, 38
Emmaeus 115f., 119

Enemies of Jesus 95f.
Evangelists 7, 20
Eyewitnesses 10

Faith 77f., 123
Family of Jesus 63, 122
Following Jesus 63, 71
Forgiveness 34, 51, 59, 113, 116

Gabriel, Angel 22, 26f.
Gentiles 16f., 105, 108
God 19, 23, 25–9, 35, 38, 48f., 112 (see
  also Kingdom of God and Holy Spirit)
Gospel 2–7 (see also Mark, Matthew and
  John)

Heaven 75, 117
Healing the sick and disabled 77–81, 119
Herod Antipas 18, 69f., 112
Holy Spirit 23, 93, 117
Homeless 58, 65
Human rights 5f.
Hume, Cardinal Basil, 122
Humility 66
Hungry 58

Isaiah, prophet 5f., 23, 41, 76, 81, 86,
  114, 118

Jesus, *passim* and particularly:
  – birth 27–32, 38
  – Christ 34f.
  – different portrait 2, 9–22
  – King 107
  – Lord 35f.
  – and lowly 27–30, 41
  – Messiah 34
  – and poor 27–30, 41–43, 58
  – Saviour 31, 33f., 38, 122

- Servant 6
- Son of God 19, 23, 25–9, 35, 38, 112
- Son of man 52f., 35, 38, 89, 112
- and women 9f., 53–7

Jeremiah, prophet 34
Jerusalem 26, 107f., 116f.
Jews 17, 25, 27f., 65–9
Joanna 115
John the Baptist 13, 23f., 41, 60, 71, 81, 98f., 116
John, Gospel of 2, 6
Joseph 26, 102, 105
Joy 117, 121
Judas Iscariot 108f., 111

Kingdom of God 41, 50, 89–95, 101

Lame persons 41, 81
Last Supper 109ff., 119
Laws 104, 119
Lepers 10, 55, 77f.
Levi 60–2
Lord's prayer 48–51, 58
Love 95f., 101, 122
Lowly persons 27–30, 41
Luke:
- a doctor? 14f.
- his character 1f.
- the date of his gospel 12
- detailed breakdown of his gospel 124–129
- as a historian 7, 10, 12–19, 27f.
- Paul's information about Luke 14
- who was he? 2, 14–16

Magnificat 27, 38, 42, 43, 58
Mark, Gospel of, 2, 6–9, 11f., 14f., 20, 41–3, 55–7, 59, 76, 78, 89, 92, 100f., 120
Martha 53f.
Mary, the mother of Jesus, 13, 22, 26–31, 35, 38, 58, 63, 102, 108, 115
Mary, the mother of James, 119
Mary, the sister of Martha, 53f.
Mary Magdalene 115, 119
Mass, see Holy Communion

Matthew, Gospel of 2, 6–9, 11, 16f., 26, 55–7, 59, 76, 83, 89
Miracles 73–81:
- catch of fishes 74
- central meaning of 81
- healing a bleeding woman 104f.
- healing a blind beggar 78
- healing a crippled woman 10, 79f., 98
- healing lepers 10
- healing a man suffering from dropsy 105
- healing a paralysed man 33f.
- loaves and fishes 75f., 97
- nature miracles 73f., 97
- raising of Jairus's daughter 33, 77
- raising of a widow's son 9f., 76, 97
- stilling a storm 73f.
Mission of the disciples 116f.
Missionaries, seventy, 17
Moorman, Bishop J. R. H., 50
Moses 24f., 30f., 33, 67, 76, 109f.

Nazareth, 5f., 27f., 105

Oral tradition 10f.
Onassis, Christina, 42–3, 121
Outcasts 52, 60f.

Parables, 10–12, 81–87, 89–93, 123 (see also Allegories and Sayings):
- banquet 90f.
- blind 82
- coin and its inscription 18
- Dives and Lazarus 10, 44–6
- good Samaritan 10, 85
- householder 90
- lost coin 52f., 83
- lost sheep 83
- prodigal son 52, 59
- ravens and lilies 83
- rich fool 10, 44
- sower 87
- tax collector 10
- tribute money 18
- vineyard 86
- waiting servants 86f.

– widow and judge 46–8
– withered fig tree 11f., 20
Pascal, Blaise, 115, 118
Passover 26f., 109f.
Persecution 65
Peter 35, 74f., 190f., 116
Pharisees 10, 54–7, 66f., 71, 83, 93, 103–5
Picasso, Pablo, 44f.
Pontius Pilate 18, 69, 111–13
Poor persons, 29–32, 41–6, 81, 95,
    98–101, 121
Prayer 46–8
Priests, Chief, 65, 67f., 112f.
Prophets 6 (see also Daniel, Isaiah,
    Jeremiah and Zechariah)
Prostitute, forgiven 54–7
Psalms 33, 35, 73f., 87, 107

Ramsey, Archbishop Michael 117
Repentance 64, 123
Resurrection 76f., 115f., 119f. (see also
    Miracles)
Rich persons 10, 41–6, 58, 95, 101, 121
Romans 12–14, 16–19, 27f., 67, 69, 71,
    111–113

Sabbath 79, 98, 103–5, 118
Sadducees 67
Samaria 64, 68, 71

Samaritans 10, 64, 68, 71, 85, 98
Sayings 87–9
Scribes 65f., 71
Second coming 92
Shepherds 30f.
Simon of Cyrene 63
Sins 34, 64, 66, 71, 83, 98, 100, 116, 121
Starving persons 51
Synagogues 66, 69, 71, 104f.

Tax collectors 10, 62, 64, 71
Temple of Jerusalem 43, 65f., 70, 72, 102,
    107f.
Temptation 51, 119
Theophilus 16
Transfiguration 24f.
Trials of Jesus 111f., 118f.

United Nations 5f.

Virgin Birth 26, 37

Woes 95, 101
Women 9f., 53–7, 121
World Council of Churches 121
Worship 117

Zacchaeus 64
Zechariah, prophet, 107

Acknowledgments

We are grateful to the following for permission to reproduce copyright material:

BBC Enterprises Ltd for the article 'Prisoners of Conscience' in *Radio Times* 10.12.88; Ewan McNaughton Associates for the article 'Mother bought drugs to wean son off habit' by Paul Stokes in *Daily Telegraph* 29.8.86, (©) The Daily Telegraph plc; The Observer Ltd for an article in *The Observer* 22.12.85; Solo Syndication & Literary Agency Ltd for the article 'Law traps fireman in the fast lane' in *Daily Mail* 29.11.88.

The Scripture quotations in this publication, unless otherwise stated, are from the Revised Standard Version of the Bible, copyrighted 1971 and 1952 by the Division of Christian Education of the National Council of the Churches of Christ in the USA.

We have been unable to trace the copyright holder in the article 'Girl hit by 20 cars on motorway' in *Daily Telegraph* 16.11.88 and would appreciate any information that would enable us to do so.

We are grateful to the following for permission to reproduce photographs:

Barnabys Picture Library, pages 24 (Hubertus Kanus), 31; Bridgeman Art Library/Private Collection, page 13; Richard Butchins, page 112; J. Allan Cash, page 28; Crisis at Christmas, page 91; Maternité, Pablo Picasso, © DACS, 1990, page 45; *The Daily Telegraph*/Peter Payne, page 79; Sally & Richard Greenhill, page 11; *The Guardian*, pages 94, 99 (Frank Martin); Daisy Hayes, pages 37, 106; Hulton-Deutsch Collection, page 72; *The Independent*/Tom Pilston, page 122–3; Clive Lawton, page 70; Network, pages 47 (Patrick Ward), 50 (Mike Goldwater), 57 *left* (Martin Mayer), 126 (Mike Goldwater); Outtake, pages 56, 57 *right*, 84; Popperfoto, pages 4 (Reuter), 43 (Reuter), 109; Rex Features/Thomas Harley, page 80; Salvation Army, page 61; Shelter Photo Library, page 30; reproduced by permission of the Stanley Spencer Estate, page 40 (Royal Academy of Arts); Topham/Press Association, page 59; Geoff Ward, pages 3, 53.

Cover:
Photographs show, Mother Teresa's Missionary of Charity, Calcutta, India, (Picturepoint) & Earth Education with ICCE Trainees & "Watch Group." (ICCE Photolibrary).

Longman Group UK Limited
Longman House, Burnt Mill, Harlow, Essex, CM20 2JE, England
and Associated Companies throughout the World.

First published 1991
ISBN 0 582 03579 1

Set in 11/12½ Rockwell Light Linotron
Produced by Longman Singapore Publishers (Pre) Ltd
Printed in Singapore